STANDING UP AGAINST HATE

To Jeanne and Doris,
my very own army women

Contents

Major General Marcia M. Anderson, U.S. Army (Ret.)

Foreword

We are more alike than we are different. That is why I am honored to introduce this book about some extraordinary African American women who defied family traditions, culture, and racial norms to join the military during World War II. These are women who, by their lives, words, and actions, prove the senselessness of disliking someone merely because of their gender, race, religion, or ethnicity.

I hope that you will share my pride in the women chronicled in these pages as you learn the story of how they excelled and succeeded in spite of significant barriers to their acceptance and full participation as members of society and the American military.

The hatred that led to the deaths of so many across the globe during World War II was, at its most basic level, the result of people who were afraid of those different than them. They were unable to accept others who did not look, speak, live, or act like themselves and, in doing so, unleashed the powerful forces of fear and ignorance. These forces existed in the United States as well as abroad.

Racism denied African Americans equal treatment in education, employment, medical care, public transportation, and voting. However, denying those basic rights did not deter the persistent strategic efforts of many throughout the African American community. They achieved advanced

educational degrees, became successful entrepreneurs, contributed to scientific research, and pursued a steady path forward for the right to full participation in the social and political fabric of the country.

Charity Adams, Alyce Dixon, the Women's Army Auxiliary Corps (WAAC) officer trainees at Fort Des Moines, the 6888th Central Postal Directory Battalion, and the thousands of African American women who served during World War II fought daily personal battles and defied long-held racial stereotypes. Their story, powerfully told in the following pages, will resonate with both old and young readers.

The women's struggles began with the high bar for acceptance as members of the WAACs. Their college degrees and professional accomplishments were often not valued by recruiters. And there were low expectations for their ability to adapt to and overcome the rigors of initial military training. They were forced to live and train in segregated facilities that were clearly substandard and unhealthy. And even after successfully completing their training, these courageous women were often not allowed to take the advanced training programs for their specialties, although they were still expected to perform clerical, medical, logistical and other tasks as well as, or even better, than white WAACs.

Their ability to overcome obstacles and exceed expectations is the reason that I, and so many others, have been able to reach the highest levels in the military. Things have changed significantly for African American women since World War II. Over the past ten years alone, we have seen several major generals and lieutenant generals in the Army, Air Force, and Navy, one of whom went on to become an admiral. Two of those women were academy graduates (Naval and West Point). Today, there are several women currently serving in command and senior-level policy positions. And the Marines just nominated a woman to be a brigadier general.

Many of the public and private opportunities that have come my way in recent years are because of my service. The biggest barrier to my success was often personal—the need to remind myself that just because I did not see anyone who looked like me in a job, that did not mean that I could not do it. This is why we must be vigilant and educate ourselves about our history. The lessons we learn from the courage and perseverance of women like Charity Adams and her colleagues convey a powerful message that when we all stand up to hate, everyone wins.

—Major General Marcia M. Anderson, Army (Ret.), May 2018

Major General Marcia M. Anderson's military career included many "firsts," from the time she was commissioned as a Second Lieutenant until she retired in 2016 after thirty-six years of service. In 2010, General Anderson became the first African American Brigadier General to serve as the Deputy Commanding General of the Army's Human Resources Command. She served in that capacity until she was selected as the first African American female Major General in the Army, Army Reserve, or Active Army, and her subsequent assignment as the Deputy Chief, Army Reserve in 2011. She has several military awards, including the Army Distinguished Service Medal as well as the Parachutists Badge.

Major Charity Adams, commander, and Captain Abbie Campbell, executive officer, inspect the 6888th Central Postal Directory Battalion in England, February 1945.

CHAPTER 1

Reporting
for War Duty

Great Britain, 1945

It was a wet, gunmetal-gray February in 1945. Rank upon rank of American khaki-clad soldiers marched down the gangplank of the *Ile de France* in Glasgow, Scotland. Newsreel cameras rolled and bagpipes played in welcome, and troops were grateful to set foot on dry land. The high, rough waves of the Atlantic had sent many soldiers running to heave their breakfasts and then to their bunks in misery. One night they had been awakened by alarm bells and the

ship's sudden erratic zigzag course, only discovering later how narrowly they had escaped a German submarine firing torpedoes at their unarmed troop ship.

The United States had galvanized all of its resources in the war against Germany, Italy, and Japan. The fight to stop these totalitarian countries from conquering the world had raged for three years, and who knew when it would end? For the first time, the United States officially allowed women to join the military. They weren't sent to battle, but they took over jobs behind the lines to free up men for combat. Thousands of American women signed up to help save democracy and preserve freedom. Yet, in America, blacks did not have the same freedom as whites. In fact, black women, and men, who joined the army were segregated into separate units.

So that day as thousands of soldiers disembarked from the *Ile de France*, one battalion was different from the rest. The 6888th Central Postal Directory Battalion was all women and all black. They were the only Women's Army Corps (WAC) unit of African American women allowed to serve overseas. Some white army officers thought they were good for nothing but scrubbing floors. And the women knew some Americans were just waiting for them to screw up.

Their commander, Major Charity Adams, was waiting when the women came off the boat. "Due to the hardships of the trip," she said, "the group was a very unhappy-looking lot." Charity, too, had a lot to prove, one of only two African

Corporal Alyce Dixon (*right*) poses with other members of the 6888th Central Postal Directory Battalion during World War II.

American women promoted to the rank of major. One of her commanding officers, a white man, had told her, "Don't let being an officer go to your head. You are still colored . . . you people have to stay in your place. Why, your folks might have been slaves to my people."

As they left the ship that day, a German V-1 rocket, known as a buzz bomb, exploded, sending the women running for cover. "It was frightening," Corporal Alyce Dixon said. "We didn't know what we had gotten ourselves into."

The WACs safely boarded the train to Birmingham, England, heading toward their first assignments. Their orders were to sort and redirect the mail to soldiers all across Europe.

The first sight of their job was a shock! Six airplane hangars, piled to the ceiling with bags of mail. Letters and packages from the States had been piling up for months.

"We were both appalled and intimidated," WAC Margaret Y. Jackson said. Nevertheless, they set right to work.

The military postal system used change-of-address cards to keep track of soldiers as they moved positions. The women had to match each letter or package with a name on a card,

Soldiers stack bags of mail to be redirected and delivered to American service personnel in Europe. Birmingham, England, 1945.

readdress it by hand, and send it on its way. To complicate the job, among the seven million American military personnel in Europe, there were thousands and thousands of duplicate names.

"Robert Smith" was popular. Seventy-five hundred men in Europe had that same name. And letters came addressed to nicknames—Bob, Rob, Bobby, Robbie, and Burt—each had to be deciphered and matched via serial number to the correct Robert.

In addition, units in battle moved so frequently some soldiers sent two or three changes of address in a single week. During the Christmas season before the women arrived, Americans had fought the biggest and bloodiest battle of the war in Europe. During the Battle of the Bulge, tens of thousands of pieces of Christmas mail had been returned from the war zone undeliverable.

"There were packages of birthday and Christmas gifts with Grandma's cookies and cakes and things . . . the food had rotted and molded," Corporal Myrtle Rhoden said. "Rats were big as cats in there."

The fighting spirit of battlefield soldiers depended on the men getting mail from home. "Letters were a great comfort. Mail was indispensable. We couldn't have won the war without it," said Lieutenant Paul Fussell, an American soldier who fought in Belgium during the Battle of the Bulge.

One moment in the Battle of the Bulge: two soldiers of the 101st Airborne running for cover in a small Belgian village not far from Bastogne to avoid being shot by a German sniper who recently killed their sergeant. Belgium, 1944.

American and British forces landed at Normandy, France, June 6, 1944. As they fought Nazi troops back toward Germany, the soldiers moved so fast, mail could not keep up with them. At the same time, every available soldier was needed for battle. Men could not be spared to redirect mail and it continued to pile up in this tiny corner in central England.

On the voyage over, the women of the 6888th heard time and again the slogan, *no mail, low morale*. They knew soldiers on the battlefield depended on them and also that their assignment was a tacit test of race relations. The unit had six months to prove themselves. They knew they could do it. ★

Major Charity Adams

CHAPTER 2

Second-Class Citizens

In the southern United States, segregation laws, referred to as Jim Crow laws, forced blacks to live separate lives from whites, never attending the same schools or using the same elevators, public bathrooms, swimming pools, or drinking fountains. Churches were for whites or blacks, but never for both, and different races couldn't even be buried in the same cemeteries.

Thousands of blacks and some whites were killed to keep African Americans from voting. Black landowners,

Some fifty thousand Ku Klux Klan members march down Pennsylvania Avenue. City officials debated whether to allow the white supremacist organization known for lynchings, violence, and terror to parade around the U.S. capital. They decided to honor the right to free speech and let them march but without their signature hoods hiding their faces. Washington, D.C., September 23, 1926.

politicians, and neighborhood leaders were assaulted in attempts to terrorize the black community into submission. Black men were murdered for as little as looking the wrong way at a white person. Those accused of killing or raping whites were often lynched without a trial. Many women in the 6888th had grown up in a segregated society, where by law they were second-class citizens with little to no chance to prove they were equal to whites.

Charity Adams had been a small child in Columbia, South Carolina, when one of the largest-ever parades of the Ku Klux Klan marched by her house. She had sat on her father's knee, watching the thousands of people walk by in their white hoods and robes. She was too young to understand this blatant racism, this expression of hate, these people who shunned, suppressed and killed others simply because of the color of their skin. But racism would

Five-year-old Charity Adams (*left*) with her cousin Rose Nash, circa 1923

be like a storm in the weather of her life, sometimes close, dark, menacing; sometimes off on the horizon, but always in the forecast.

Charity's parents taught her to avoid confrontation with whites but also to believe in herself, no matter what anyone said.

She was the oldest of four siblings, and education was important in the Adams family. She made good grades, becoming the valedictorian at Booker T. Washington High School. Her mother was a stickler for proper grammar. When Charity went

away to Wilberforce University in Ohio and wrote home, her mother corrected mistakes in the letters with a red pen. After college Charity returned to her hometown in South Carolina to teach high school math and science in the same segregated school system she had attended. After four years of teaching, she decided to go to graduate school and study vocational psychology at Ohio State University. That's what she was doing when Japan attacked Pearl Harbor, Hawaii, launching the United States into what would become World War II.

"If you lived during the bombing of Pearl Harbor, it was like a bolt of lightning," said Gladys Schuster Carter. "Everybody had to do something; men volunteered and were later drafted, women worked in factories, everybody wanted to do their part." But neither Gladys nor Charity would have predicted they would join the U. S. Army.

Women in the army! Some Americans thought it was scandalous; some thought it went against nature. When Congresswoman Edith Nourse Rogers first introduced the idea in the spring of 1941 before Pearl Harbor, the bill was dead before it hit the floor. Then America joined Great Britain and France, the Allied forces fighting for democracy. They opposed the Axis nations—Germany, Italy, and Japan—which were ruled by fascist governments focused on military expansion. America desperately needed more army troops, and women taking over noncombat positions would free up men for battle.

Army leaders decided to work with Congresswoman Rogers on legislation to form the Women's Army Auxiliary Corps (WAAC). Also crafting the bill were Eleanor Roosevelt, wife of President Franklin D. Roosevelt, and Doctor Mary McLeod Bethune, founder of the National Council of Negro Women and adviser to the president on African American affairs.

The notion of women in the military provoked stirring debate. In the early 1940s, most Americans believed the proper course for young women was marriage, raising children, and working at home. This wasn't a reality for most black women, many of whom had to work low-paying service jobs while raising their families. But the prevailing American attitude was that women did not have the capacity to handle the serious business of the work world, let alone the military.

"This war is not teas, dances, card parties, and amusements," argued Congressman Clare Eugene Hoffman of Michigan in opposing the bill. "You take a poll of the honest-to-goodness women at home, the women who have families, the women who sew on the buttons, do the cooking, mend the clothing, do the washing, and you will find there is where they want to stay—in the homes."

Congress approved the Women's Auxiliary Army Corps,* and it was signed into law on May 14, 1942. As auxiliary members of the army, women would not earn equal pay to

---

* Congress converted the auxiliary corps to the regular army on July 3, 1943, creating the Women's Army Corps (WAC).

Mary K. Adair takes an examination for Officers' Candidate School, Fort McPherson, Georgia, June 20, 1942.

men in the military. They had no military rank or entitlements for dependents, but it was a start, and throughout the process Dr. Bethune had lobbied for African American women to participate equally in this historic breakthrough for women.

Black leaders saw wartime as an opportunity to push for change. African American men were already volunteering for service and being drafted into the military, albeit a segregated military. Their manpower would be essential for victory, and equal participation in the military could dismantle segregation. But was it logical to fight for democracy in Europe when legal discrimination barred blacks from voting in some states? Should lives be risked abroad while

Oveta Culp Hobby is sworn in as the first WAAC by Major General Myron C. Cramer. General George C. Marshall (*second from left*) and Secretary of War Henry L. Stimson were among witnesses to the ceremony, May 16, 1942.

racism remained a deadly enemy at home? The *Pittsburgh Courier*, an African American newspaper, organized the "Double V" campaign, and across the nation blacks rallied to the motto, "Democracy: Victory at home, Victory abroad."

In meetings with Eleanor Roosevelt, Dr. Bethune put forth a strong case for integration of the WAAC, but the official U.S. policy stood. Although prohibiting discrimination, it permitted segregation with the twisted logic of separate but equal. Dr. Bethune convinced Eleanor Roosevelt that African American women should be permitted to train as officers,

just like white women. Eleanor's influence swayed the War Department to agree. Across the ranks, men and women, the War Department called for 10 percent enlistment of blacks; and in the first WAAC Officer Candidate School of four hundred forty women, forty spots would be open to African Americans. This 10 percent represented the blacks in the nation's civilian population.

The word went out across the country through black universities, churches, and community organizations. Dr. Bethune wanted the best and brightest women to become those first African American WAAC officers.

Charity Adams, now age twenty-three, received a letter of invitation. Her college friends from her days at Wilberforce University in Ohio, which was a historically black college, had urged her not to give up her teaching future for a questionable job in the military. But she was restless. Teaching high school math and science had become dull, rigid and offered her no challenges. A black woman in the South, even with a college degree, faced a limited future. The WAAC looked like an opportunity; Charity applied, was accepted, and became one of the first women to volunteer.

"Even with the knowledge that there were many other women receiving notices like mine, how special I felt! Not that the army had done me any favor by accepting me, but rather that the army had gone to the trouble to find me and to want all that I had to offer."

A little more than a month later, she was sworn in. "That is when the fear set in. What had I gotten myself into?" Charity wondered. But now her friends stepped up to support her. "Had it not been for my friends, I think I would have backed out."

Shortly thereafter, July 19, 1942, Charity bounced along in the back of an army truck with a group of women recruits headed to Fort Des Moines Training Center, Iowa. The women,

Press coverage by the *Afro-American* of the first black women to report for training in the WAAC. Fort Des Moines, Iowa, August 1, 1942.

black and white, lurched, bumped, and tumbled against one another as the truck took a curve. They had left home and everything familiar. Riding the overnight train together through four states, they felt some closeness. Charity shared a berth in their Pullman car with a white woman who had been sworn in at the same time with her at Fort Hayes, Ohio.

"Race, color, age, finances, social class had been pushed aside," Charity said. Travel weary and anxious, none of them

nent, Women's Army Auxiliary Corps

knew what to expect. The dreary rain splashing down might have temporarily dampened their enthusiasm, but the women had struck out on an adventure. Together they would become the first officers in the WAAC. They would prove that women could make it in the army.

The army truck rattled through the gates of Fort Des Moines and stopped with one last jerk. Charity and the other women carefully climbed down, stepping into the mud. The two dozen new WAAC recruits were directed to line up by twos and walk to the mess hall. In the army, breakfast, lunch, and dinner were called mess. They ate their first meal surrounded by reporters and news cameras.

"I, a Negro, had my picture on the front page of a white daily without having done anything criminal," Charity said. "A most unusual situation."

After mess they marched to the reception center. An officer pointed to a far group of seats. "Will all the colored girls move over to this side?"

There was a moment of stunned silence. "It did not occur to us that this could happen," Charity said. "Worse was . . . after the 'colored girls' had been pushed to the side . . . the white women were called by name to be led to their quarters." Charity wondered, "Why could not the 'colored girls' be called by name?" Segregation implied inferiority, causing the women resentment and an inescapable feeling of shame.

When the black women had settled into their quarters, the commander apologized to them. Segregation wasn't his idea, he said. He was just following army policy. Charity Adams would hear these words again and again during her years in the service, each time a piercing insult. ★

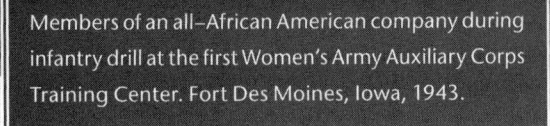

Members of an all–African American company during infantry drill at the first Women's Army Auxiliary Corps Training Center. Fort Des Moines, Iowa, 1943.

CHAPTER 3

Becoming Officers Together

Fort Des Moines, Iowa, August 1942

Two sisters, Leader and Nealie Hoskins, were inspired to volunteer for WAAC officer training because their grandfather had been a soldier in World War I. Because they were the first sisters to join the U.S. Army, their picture ran in newspapers around the world. But the night they arrived at Fort Des Moines and marched in to dinner, they discovered large signs bearing the word "colored" relegating them to tables at the far end of the mess hall. One white woman from Georgia didn't even want them in the same room.

Captain Dovey Johnson, 1942

"I've never eaten with a Negro, and I'm not going to start now," she announced.

The women went through the line and got plates of food, but then Leader, Nealie, and a number of other black women upended their plates on the table and marched out. They bought dinner at the Post Exchange [army general store] and ate in their barracks, debating whether they should leave the army before they even started—though they didn't have much choice. Once you join the army, it's a crime to leave before you are officially discharged.

Dovey Johnson, a black officer candidate from Charlotte, North Carolina, said, "With those signs on the tables, and the [American] flags outside, something's wrong."

"Everyone felt depressed, broken and betrayed," said Dovey. "We had come expecting there would be one corps. One. Not two. There was definitely two."

The women took turns using the one telephone available to confer with friends and family and try to reach their advocate, Dr. Mary McLeod Bethune.

"We cried, we didn't sleep," Dovey said. They drank coffee and waited for an explanation from the army. A day and a half later, a white WAAC officer met with them.

"She tried to explain America is segregated. That's how life is," Dovey said. "I argued with her. 'No, no, no, you can't tell me that. I been all over the United States. I haven't seen that. I haven't read about it. . . . Have they changed the Constitution?' Everybody laughed and that at least gave relief, but I didn't say it as a joke."

Dovey figured she would be booted out of the army. "Very definitely. Because I was loud and wronged. I was hurt. I was hurt to the core."

Alerted to the problem, Dr. Bethune, Eleanor Roosevelt, and WAAC Chief Colonel Oveta Culp Hobby came to Fort Des Moines to see about the situation. "Mrs. Hobby, [who was white] told the white girls that we had enlisted just like they had, to do the same job," Leader said. "And we should be given the same kind of treatment."

The "colored" signs disappeared from the mess hall, but segregation remained. The black women would have to live with it. Dr. Bethune told them, "We are making history here today. The Negro women whose faces are turned this way are depending upon you to represent us on the ground floor of this dramatic new program . . . Out of millions of us, you have been selected . . . [for a] grave responsibility—a challenging responsibility."

Chief Colonel Oveta Culp Hobby (*right*) meets with Mrs. Mary McLeod Bethune (*left*) to discuss training African American women auxiliaries. Mrs. Bethune was in charge of black WAACs at Fort Des Moines, July 21, 1942.

"She . . . told us that they [the War Department] did not want us in the service in the first place," said officer trainee Abbie Noel Campbell. "So we had to set an example. And we did. We did a beautiful job."

The black women were also inspired by the call issued by Colonel Hobby during their training: "From now on you are soldiers, defending a free way of life . . . You wear the uniform of the army of the United States. Respect the uniform. Respect all that it stands for."

Years later, Leader Hoskins chuckled remembering, "A funny thing happened at the end of our training. Everybody hugged each other goodbye—including that girl from Georgia."

Army life required a huge adjustment for all the women. A cannon blast and bugle call woke them at five o'clock in the morning, but the lack of privacy in the barracks was even harder to get used to.

"You got down to your birthday suit," said one woman. "I hid myself behind the bedposts, bunk posts, and exposed only my backside."

The barracks were two floors of large rooms, each with ten to eighteen women. The bathrooms in the basement had communal showers. If nobody hogged the sinks, they could all be on time for half-past-six reveille, the bugle notes that signaled the morning roll call. After that they cleaned the barracks and made their beds before breakfast.

In the army, there was a time for everything, a place for everything, and a regulation way to do everything. Regular inspections made sure everybody followed directions precisely. When making their beds, the fold in the top sheet had to be two inches from the bottom of the pillow and exactly six inches deep. The sheets and blankets were folded precisely at each corner and had to be smooth and tight across the bed.

Charity feared she wouldn't make her bed correctly. Every night for the first week, she squirmed between the sheets,

New WAAC recruits of the Thirty-Second Company stand at attention during inspection of their barracks by Commanding Officer Frances D. Alexander, accompanied by First Lieutenant Violet W. (Hill) Askins. Fort Huachuca, Arizona, December 5, 1942.

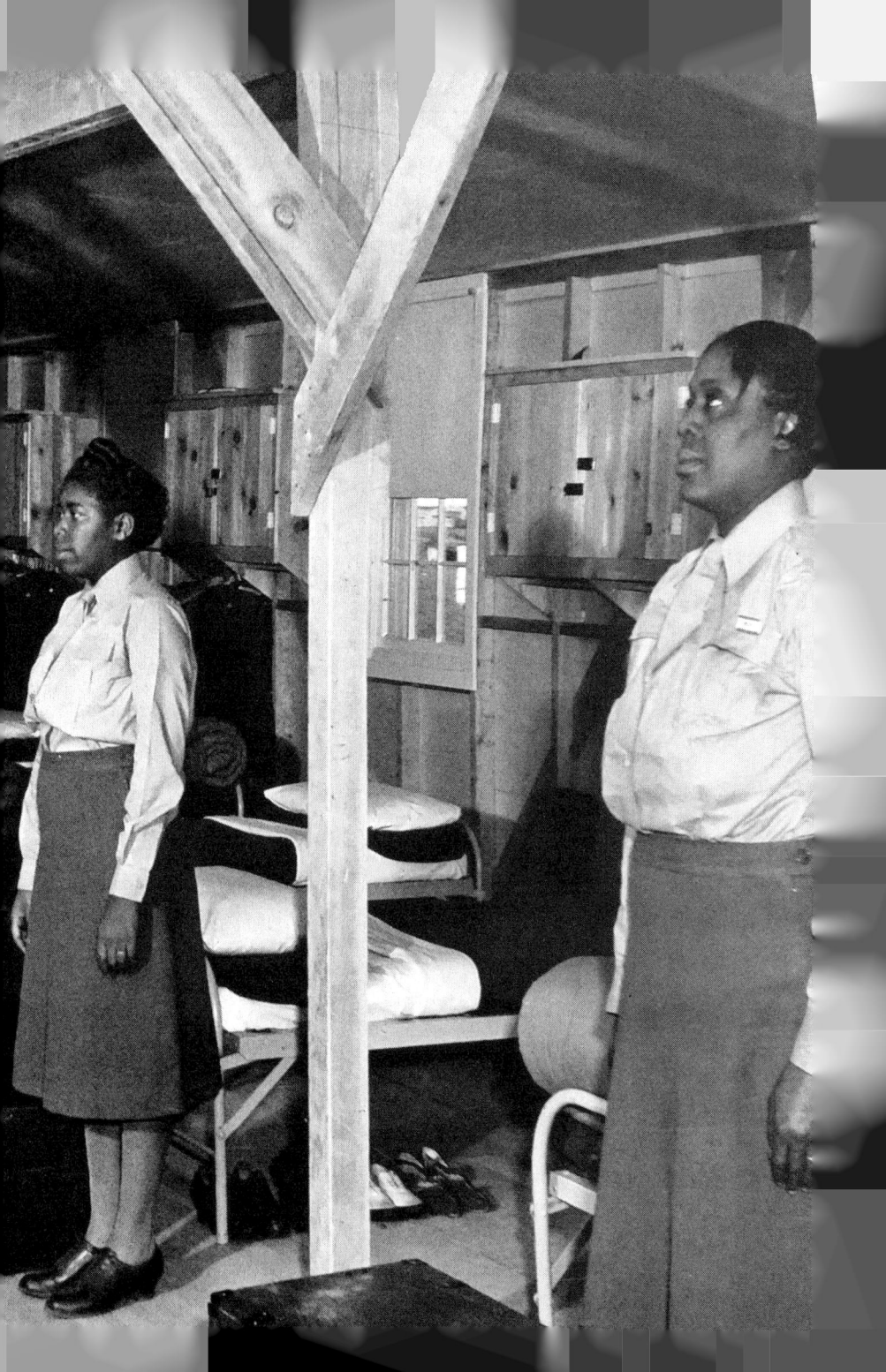

keeping them tucked in, trying to sleep without moving, then slithering out in the morning. The inspecting officer grew suspicious and asked to see Charity make her own bed. Luckily, it wasn't as hard as she feared.

Each woman stowed all her belongings in two lockers, a low one at the foot of her bed and a tall one at the head. There was little room for anything except military gear, and from underwear to overcoat, it had to be stored precisely according to regulation.

Dovey thrilled to the starched khaki, the spit and polish, and smart saluting of the flag. She embraced the message of the newsreels they watched touting the "Four Freedoms" for which America was fighting: freedom of speech, freedom of worship, freedom from want, and freedom from fear.

"I discovered in those first months at Fort Des Moines a force greater than the army's attempt to divide us. That was our common belief in the war. Black and white alike, we anguished over the grim newspaper accounts of the endless string of Allied defeats in Europe, in North Africa, in Russia. When our boys began turning the tide against the Japanese in Guadalcanal in August [1942], we celebrated together."

The WAACs detected some resentment on the part of the men at Fort Des Moines whose duty it was to turn the women into soldiers. "But what they didn't know is women are determined," Dovey said. "And we stayed up late nights studying those manuals."

Black and white officer candidates were formed into platoons of forty women. The platoon of black women was assigned to a company including two platoons of white women. The one hundred twenty women went to class together, studying military courtesy and army organization, first aid, current events, map reading, and what to do if the enemy attacked by air or with chemicals. Every day they turned out for physical training and drilled together, learning to stand at attention, march with precision, and when and how to salute.

Recruits Vera Campbell of New York City and Glendora Moore of Washington, D.C., make themselves at home in their barracks. Fort Huachuca, December 1942.

"We saluted like *mad*," Charity said, "indoors and outdoors, at the proper time and improper time, to the right people and to the wrong people. And there were times when we had no idea what to do."

Some army men shook their heads at the sight of women learning basic infantry drill, but rain or shine the women formed up on the parade ground to practice. They marched to the classroom, to drill, to mess, a constant *fall in, attention, straighten those shoulders, belly in, hut two, forward march, halt, fall out, dismissed*, from morning to night.

Charity Adams identified herself on this postcard showing new WAAC officer candidates performing their daily physical training. "I did not like physical training . . . I had never been particularly athletic, and, suddenly, I was required to successfully execute handsprings and push-ups. I managed the latter after several weeks of effort. It was a major accomplishment when I did seven push-ups without falling down."

CALISTHENICS—WAAC FT. DES MOINES

1st Co., 1st Regt., July + August 1942 (OCS)

"I took to drill the way a duck takes to water," Charity said. "I read the manual and practiced. I joined any group on the field and quoted the manual to help others correct their movements." One day at drill, she volunteered to give the commands.

"I took my place three paces to the left of the platoon, and in my loudest voice I gave a command. Not one foot moved, and the lieutenant training the group called out, 'Miss Adams, did I hear someone say something?'"

When dismissed for the evening, she and some classmates went to the parade ground and practiced their "command voices" until dark. "That's the night I learned to speak from the diaphragm," Charity said. "Ever since then I have been able to make myself heard."

Three weeks into training, a newspaper reporter who viewed the black WAACs drilling wrote they marched "with heads high" and "firm of step . . . breathing defiance to Hitler, Hirohito, and Mussolini."

Black and white women often studied together in their off time and Charity became friends with some of the white women. On their day off the WAACs could take a trolley into the city of Des Moines to see a movie, shop, or try local restaurants. Black WAACs were invited to local churches and befriended by Des Moines families.

Day by day the women became soldiers, used to being told what to do, what to wear and when, tying neckties, shining

shoes, and jumping-to at every whistle or bugle call. Nevertheless, even dressed alike and marching in step, segregation never let Charity forget that in the eyes of the army she was second-class.

One day, after a gas mask drill, everyone lined up to clean their masks, wiping them with disinfectant. The line halted when a white WAAC announced she would not use the same cleaning cloth as a black WAAC.

"Everyone turned to look, but no one stepped forward to offer another cloth." Charity said. "There was no way to know . . . how many kinds of disinfectants she used on her mask for the next drill."

WAAC recruits participate in a gas mask drill.

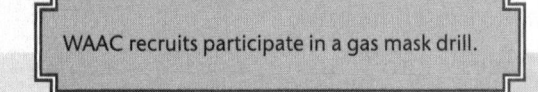

In this atmosphere, Charity found it difficult to be optimistic about her future. Asked her choice of assignment, she chose truck driver, hoping to avoid becoming a cook.

Graduation day finally arrived. Excited and happy to survive six weeks of training, the WAACs stood and pronounced their oath of office. In alphabetical order, Charity Adams topped the roster. But she had to wait for all four hundred white women to be commissioned before she became the first Negro woman officer in the WAAC. Still, Charity was proud of her accomplishment.

"Whatever doubts we might have later," she said, "we put on our gold bars and . . . that day we knew ourselves as members of the great fraternity of officers." ★

Third Officer Charity Edna Adams receives her commission from Major General Frederick E. Uhl. Fort Des Moines, August 29, 1942.

CHAPTER 4

Black Women Persist

After commissioning came assignments. Lieutenant Charity Adams did not end up a truck driver. Like most of the new officers, she was assigned command of enlisted women who arrived for basic training. Most enlistees were white women, however, and army policy forbade blacks to command whites. For several months, black officers outnumbered the black enlistees trickling in. Charity and the other black officers took turns training them, while also learning the other duties necessary to running a company of enlisted soldiers.

Lieutenant Dovey Johnson was assigned to recruiting and sent to the states of Georgia, Florida, and North and South Carolina to convince black women to join the army. The word was out that the WAAC was segregated. Dovey feared the small gains she and other African American WAAC officers had made would be lost if more black women did not volunteer.

"That, I determined, would not happen—not on my watch, no matter how tough a sell I had on my hands in pitching a Jim Crow WAAC in the Deep South." Dovey believed in the critical role of women in the war effort, and she believed the WAAC was a step forward for African Americans.

"Was that opportunity precisely, mathematically, documentable equal to that of whites? Probably not. But the WAAC offered a chance I believed would never come again in quite the same way: the chance to advance, to train for careers, to build the kind of future we women wanted for our children, to stand behind the men who were fighting in Europe and North Africa and the Pacific. That mattered most of all. Our boys were *dying* for freedom, I pointed out in every speech I made. What was segregation compared to that?"

Even as she recruited, Dovey suspected black woman were being eliminated before they applied. Earlier that summer when she had gone to pick up her own WAAC application at the post office in Charlotte, North Carolina, "they told me that they didn't know anything about it," Dovey said. But she

had inside information. She knew the WAAC was required by law to admit black women. Dr. Mary McLeod Bethune was a family friend, and Dovey had worked in her office, privy to discussions between Dr. Bethune and Eleanor Roosevelt during drafting of the WAAC legislation.

"I'm sitting there with the very bill still with the ink kind of moist on it," Dovey said. She called Dr. Bethune, who advised her to move farther north and try again. Dovey went to stay with relatives in Richmond, Virginia, and in that town, she was allowed to apply.

Mary Elnora White said when she tried to apply at a recruiting office, she was sent on a "wild goose chase" by white personnel who claimed the recruiter was "unavailable" every time she visited the office. She wrote the War Department, complaining this type of racism was no better than Nazi Germany, "the very thing the Allies are fighting against."

In the first week WAAC recruitment offices opened, the army discovered five cities were not following the rules. They were turning away black applicants. Recruiters in Pittsburgh, Pennsylvania, Winston-Salem, North Carolina, Columbia, South Carolina, Dallas, Texas, and St. Paul, Minnesota, were sent telegraphs ordering them to correct this. Throughout the war, the army continued to receive numerous complaints about recruiters turning away African American women.

Once a woman did get an application and completed it, she then had to pass an interview, a physical, and the

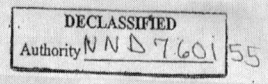

Here I am, for instance, ready to offer my very life the only thing I have to offer, if necessary in an effort to do my part in this gigantic struggle for the preservation of democracy and the high ideals that we all cherish so highly against totalitarianism and brutality. This is not a white man's war, it is not a black man's war, but it is a war in which all of us must participate, must put all of our efforts, our genius, into, in order to successfully combat the enemy. And it will take both white & colored to do this. You cannot do it by yourself. Nor can we. It is a cinch: Together we stand, divided

Page four of a seven-page letter from Mary Elnora White of Paducah, Kentucky, to the U.S. War Department. "Here I am, for instance, ready to give my very life, the only thing I have to offer, if necessary in an effort to do my part in this gigantic effort for the preservation of democracy."

Mental Alertness Test (MAT). The MAT was another hurdle for black women because it was designed with a bias toward middle-class Americans of European descent.

One psychologist on the WAAC applicant reviewing board said some African American women demonstrated excellent leadership material, but the MAT misjudged them "because it called for general information which was not part of their particular background." ·

WAAC headquarters initially sent Dovey and several other African American women on recruiting trips, where they spoke at black churches, colleges, YWCAs, and NAACP meetings. The War Department received complaints from some communities about African American women recruiters "in public places giving public speeches," as if this should not be allowed. Less than a year later, the corps pulled most African American recruiting officers from the field, claiming a shortage of personnel.

Even so, hundreds of African American women enlisted in the WAAC. Ruby Lee Seals Carvin, of Houston, Texas, was walking along feeling badly because she couldn't afford to go to college, when she happened to see a billboard. On it, a stern-eyed Uncle Sam pointed his long finger and demanded, "I want you!"

"I felt like he was talking to me," Ruby said. "[In the army] I could save my money for college, and do something for my country, too." Ruby quit her job at the ticket window of a local theater and joined up.

Bernice Thomas, of Harlem, New York, was a single parent working a boring, repetitive job pressing underwear in the garment district when she decided to enlist. "I felt that women in the military were going to have a better opportunity when everything was over and there would be jobs opening up, particularly for black women." A number of women left children with relatives to enlist.

Mary Daniels Williams, of Cleveland, Ohio, had dropped out of school after the ninth grade and worked cleaning houses. "I was going nowhere fast. I could see us living in the slums forever," she said. Mary decided to talk to an army recruiter at a post office in Cincinnati. "They promised us education, new places to go and to visit—well, just a totally new life."

Black recruits had a variety of backgrounds and education. Charity Adams had finished college and one year of graduate school. Some women had only a fourth grade reading level, others held doctorate degrees. Many African American women, especially those from the South, had gone to second-rate schools without the books, playgrounds, or activities equal to white children.

The women were smart, capable, and eager to learn. As they neared the end of basic training, the women took the Army General Classification Test, gauging soldiers' knowledge

of language, math, and spatial relations. Scores on the test indicated how readily recruits might learn the facts, skills, and techniques needed for army duties.

WAACs who scored high enough on the test went to specialist school and trained to be secretaries, office managers, cooks and bakers, physical therapists, medical technicians, and code breakers. Women in the motor transportation school learned to drive army vehicles, including the quarter-ton jeep and one-and-a-half-ton trucks used to carry troops and supplies. They learned motor mechanics and inspected all vehicles before they were driven from the motor pool. Women who scored lower on the classification test were assigned unskilled jobs like cleaning, or carrying and stacking supplies.

White WAACs were more often sent to training school, while many black women received no training beyond basic. African American women were completely barred from training for physical therapy and code breaking.

"I wanted to go to motor corps to drive a truck," said WAAC Ernestine Woods. After graduation, she waited nervously as the officers called out assignments for the motor corps. Her name wasn't called.

Next, names were read for office work. "Again, I waited anxiously and breathlessly," said Ernestine. Her heart sank when she didn't hear her name, and she began to pray. The only school left was cooks and bakers. Ernestine did not want a kitchen job. Once again, her name wasn't called.

These WAACs, thoroughly trained in the handling of all types of trucks, are awaiting the command to start their vehicles at the post motor pool. Fort Huachuca, December 8, 1942.

She had mixed feelings, "happy not to be on the list [for kitchen work] but sad to think nobody wanted us [black WAACs]. We went back to our bunks and cried."

WAAC Mary Rozier felt lucky to be picked for administration school. She knew "a lot of girls who were teachers [in civilian life] were sent to cooks' and bakers' school."

But even specialized training did not guarantee a black woman would get an assignment. The army's segregation policy made it difficult because some forts didn't have room to segregate blacks and whites. Worse yet, some post commanders refused outright to take African American WAACs. And even if a black woman had the chance to complete training and get assigned to a post, her actual duties were decided by white male officers.

Throughout the war years, Colonel Oveta Culp Hobby would try to appease both sides, telling African American leaders and newspapers that black women were treated equally, while at the same time assuring concerned whites that the army was maintaining segregation. She dealt with a number of complaints from southern congressmen and citizens about segregation breaking down at Fort Des Moines.

"I would appreciate a letter from you on the subject," wrote Representative George Mahon, Democrat from Texas, passing on a complaint from a constituent about a white WAAC "now

forced to share the same living quarters, bathroom facilities, restrooms, and reception rooms with n—."

Colonel Hobby tried to deflect this type of criticism, answering that contact between African American and white servicewomen was kept at a minimum, but some contact was "temporary and practically unavoidable." Her response to blacks about the unfairness of segregation followed official U.S. military policy. It stated the army was not the place to resolve social issues, and especially not while the country was fighting a foreign war.

It fell to officers like Charity Adams to encourage the black recruits, build their confidence, and give them hope. In December 1942, Charity was promoted straight from third to first officer, called captain. She gained much satisfaction from seeing a group of civilian women arrive under her command and see them leave six weeks later as well-trained troops.

"I knew there was no such thing as separate but equal," Charity said, "but I had become determined to see that any troops I commanded would have every opportunity that was afforded others. I knew that there was no such thing as personal success, that success came only if we all succeeded together."

Both black and nonblack WAACs had husbands, fiancés, or brothers in the armed forces, and they wanted to hasten the war's end. In the words of one WAAC newsletter, they

WAAC Captain Charity Adams drills her company on the drill ground at the first WAAC Training Center. Fort Des Moines, May 1943.

marched and sweated and drilled—to stand "in the place of the man behind the gun."

"There are, I am persuaded, places within the human heart where no system can reach," said Dovey Johnson. "At Fort Des Moines, we found them . . . Conversations begun in the open air had a way of spilling over into the mess hall . . . Once the mess hall signs came down, so did the invisible line, quietly enough that the commandant chose to look the other way as first one girl, and then another broke the color line . . . What grew up with astonishing speed, overall, was a camaraderie that pushed and pressed its way between the cracks of army regulations on the base."

Black women wanted to serve their country and demonstrate their patriotism. They saw the army as an opportunity to better their life, find adventure, or see the world. Thousands applied for service, took the required tests, and by the end of World War II, 6,520 black women would serve in the U.S. Army. ★

WAACs arrive at Fort Huachuca, Arizona, and carry their belongings into the barracks. Fort Huachuca was home to some ten thousand African American servicemen training for duty, and the WAACs' arrival was met with great excitement, December 1942.

CHAPTER 5

Every Victory Counts

Fort Huachuca, Arizona, December 1942

The first two companies of black WAACs finished basic training at Fort Des Moines and were assigned to an all-black army post. Taking a troop train, they headed west from Iowa to a remote army post edging the Sonoran Desert near Tombstone, Arizona. Fort Huachuca was home to some ten thousand African American servicemen training for duty, including the Ninety-Second and Ninety-Third Army Infantry Divisions.

Thousands of the men turned out at the depot, cheering the women as they stepped off the train. The Thirty-Second and Thirty-Third WAAC companies, about one hundred fifty women, took up duties, as the men of the Ninety-Second were deployed overseas to combat zones.

The women settled into their new home, confident they could "soldier with the best men." They brought various skills and experience. Hulda DeFreese of Hillburn, New York, with a fine arts degree from New York University, worked

A Christmas dance at Negro Service Club No. 3 sponsored by the 1323rd Engineers. They had their own orchestra. Camp Swift, Texas, December 23, 1943.

WAACs Ruth Wade (*left*) and Lucille Mayo demonstrate their ability to service trucks as taught them during the processing period at Fort Des Moines and put into practice at Fort Huachuca. December 8, 1942.

as a cartographer drawing contour maps of the terrain surrounding Fort Huachuca. The maps were vital for the soldiers on maneuvers in the mountains. Eleanor Bracey, a chemist, from Toledo, Ohio, had one of the most important duties on the base in the sewage disposal and water purification plant. Lucia Pitts replaced a male sergeant major in the provost marshal's office, supervising the office administration and one hundred fifty military police.

These WAACs are shown the intricacies of the Fort Huachuca switchboard by the enlisted men operators whom they will replace. Already efficient operators because of their training at Fort Des Moines, they need only be taught the post routine before taking over the operation. December 8, 1942.

At Fort Huachuca, all positions approved for women by the War Department were open to blacks. WAACs were typists, stenographers, and clerks; they did light truck maintenance, drove vehicles, and worked as chauffeurs, messengers, telephone operators, and librarians. They ran the theaters and service clubs and served as medical, laboratory, and surgical technicians and hospital ward attendants.

When they had been on duty at Fort Huachuca about six months, the post commander Colonel Edwin N. Hardy said, "These young women are showing marked ability and genius in taking over essential jobs from able-bodied men."

Fort Riley, Kansas, 1943

The second largest group of African American WAACs deployed stateside took up duty at Fort Riley, Kansas, in late August 1943. The commander was glad to have them and assigned the women to the post hospital as ward orderlies, ward attendants, nurses' aides, physiotherapy aids, and medical, surgical, dental, and laboratory technicians and to the hospital mess.

Walla Walla Army Air Base, Washington State, 1943

Army air force bases also requisitioned black women, and a group of more than seventy-five WAACs was sent to Walla Walla Army Air Base in Washington State. A week after their arrival, the local press reported the graduates of the WAAC administration or cooking and baking schools at Fort Des Moines were satisfied with their assignments. Other WAACs took up clerical duties at base headquarters or technical jobs at the base hospital, photographic laboratory, or ordinance department. Others worked as sheet metal workers and parachute inspectors.

Seven weeks after their tour of duty had begun in Walla Walla, the base commander, Lieutenant Colonel Harry E.

Gilmore said "The spirit of the WACs on this base is best evidenced by the fact that all of the original company reenlisted for the duration . . . These girls are intelligent and capable workers, and a credit to the uniform which they wear [and] they are fast becoming an invaluable aid to the officers and departments throughout the base command."

Second Lieutenant Martha S. Putney served in the U.S. Women's Army Corps from February 1943 to December 1946.

> WAACs of the Thirty-Second and Thirty-Third Companies dine in a segregated mess hall, 1942.

A smaller black WAC unit deployed to Douglas Army Air Field in Arizona was put to work packing parachutes and assisting with aircraft maintenance

Fort Des Moines, Iowa, 1943

Martha S. Putney, from Norristown, Pennsylvania, joined a later officer training class at Fort Des Moines in the spring of 1943. By now, in the mess hall the signs indicating tables for blacks and nonblacks were gone, but black and white WAAC

companies marched into meals single file, got their trays and sat down in order, so they automatically ended up segregated. But on Saturday and Sunday, they didn't march into the mess hall in formation, and Martha wanted to make a point.

"We decided that we were just going to sit anywhere we wanted in the mess hall on those two days. And the first Saturday we did it, a couple of the non-blacks picked up their trays and moved . . . We talked about it ahead of time, and not only our company, but by Sunday . . . every black company got the message." Martha expected they might be reprimanded, but they were not. "Saturday and Sunday were desegregation days. That's what we called them."

The swimming pool at Fort Des Moines was also segregated. African American women were given one hour on Friday afternoons to swim, and as soon as they left the water, the pool was cleansed and "purified." "If I'd ever had to watch that heinous process," said Dovey Johnson, "I might have resigned."

Again Martha Putney saw an opening for change and jumped in. She commanded a company of black women within a training unit that also contained companies of white women. They were mistakenly all assigned the same swimming hours.

"When can we swim?" The black women asked her.

"Swim with your unit," Martha said.

"What?"

"Look, I'm ordering you to swim with your unit." Martha said, "They knew what an order was. They swam with their unit. When that happened all the rest of the people saw what was happening. They began to swim when they wanted to, when the pool wasn't full. I broke down desegregation—I desegregated the swimming pool at Fort Des Moines and to my knowledge, as long as I was there, it was still desegregated."

Captain Charity Adams's leadership and organizational skills continued to grow as she guided fresh troops through basic training and took on more responsibility for operations at Fort Des Moines. She developed a personal code for when

Lieutenant Ernestine Wood (*far right*) presenting a check for money raised in a war bond drive. Chicago, Illinois, May 1945.

she bumped up against institutional racism: step sideways if you must, but never retreat. One example was the Negro WAC Band. For some time Charity sent any qualified woman in her company to audition for the WAC Band. Some were school music teachers, others teaching or performance majors in college or graduate school, and some were even amateur and professional musical performers. Regardless of their experience, no black women who auditioned were selected for the band.

Charity and other African American officers decided to organize their own marching and concert band. Fort Des Moines received many requests for military band appearances and sent the black women's band to play at patriotic events such as bond drives. War bonds issued by the U.S. government helped pay the costs of the war.

"I don't think anybody ever heard of a black women's military band before, and that to us was really something," said Lieutenant Ernestine White, one of the band's leaders. "As a matter of fact, most people had never seen black women in uniform before."

Charity Adams was assigned to travel with the band and give speeches appealing to citizens to purchase war bonds. Available in denominations of one thousand dollars down to twenty-five dollars, they were affordable for everyone. People could also buy war stamps for ten cents. These were especially popular with children who placed the stamps in

special albums. When full, the albums were redeemed for a bond.

Riding in an uncomfortable army bus with instruments piled in the back, the WAC Band crisscrossed the state of Iowa, playing music in the bandstands of small town squares, sometimes three stops in one day. As the musicians' tune-up notes soared into the air, townspeople emerged from nearby buildings or drove up and parked to listen. After noontime concerts, citizens shared a picnic lunch with band members.

Many of the towns where the black band played had no black residents. Corporal Clementine McConico Skinner of Illinois, who played the French horn and trumpet, said wherever they went they were received graciously, and treated as if they belonged. "They made us feel like celebrities. Many of the young girls sought our autographs as if we were famous."

They also marched in parades and played for veterans at a hospital in Des Moines. The band performed concerts twice a month at the fort theater and started a dance band and a jazz combo that played at the service club. "On Saturday nights," said Private First Class Audrey Gross, "We had a swing band and those white girls would come over to our barracks . . . because they said our music was jazzier than theirs."

On July 10, 1944, the 404th WAC Band was made official and some members promoted in rank. They traveled for a concert at an annual NAACP conference in Chicago, marched

The 404th WAC Band marching in Chicago, May 30, 1945

in a parade, and gave an outdoor concert. When they arrived back at Fort Des Moines they were shocked to find their band would be dissolved. They were the only all-women's African American band in the U.S. army, and now all members would be reclassified and sent to different units. The order came as part of an army wide cutback in the number of military bands.

The news stunned Clementine but not so much that she couldn't fight back. She organized band members to launch a letter-writing campaign. The women targeted both black and nonblack leaders at the local and national levels protesting deactivation of the band. For fear of reprisals, they left the fort to mail their letters in the city of Des Moines.

Black newspapers across the country picked up the campaign, publishing letters of protest. One read: "To disband now the Negro band which was . . . formed as a compromise measure adds insult to injury and will be a serious blow to the morale of the Negro WACs."

The army claimed there were not enough personnel stationed at Fort Des Moines to warrant two bands. A flood of letters and phone calls to the War Department demanded that the army either reactivate the band and restate its members or allow black WACs to join the white band and continue as army musicians. Unwilling to integrate the white unit, the War Department announced August 16, 1944, the black WAC band would be reactivated due to its importance in boosting morale.

Though segregated, the 404th WAC band and its success became a point of pride for the African American WACs. They grasped opportunity and encouragement where they could find it. Clementine enjoyed the honor of playing taps for black troops each night, signaling the end of the day. She found it inspiring telling soldiers to go to sleep and watching "lights go out on the post on a star-studded night." ★

WAAC bugler at Fort Huachuca, Arizona

6 WACs Resign

WAC Clerks Decline to Scrub Floors

War Department Admits Girls Were Improperly Assigned

WAACS CHANGED TO WACS NOW

Disturbance Follows Soldier's Attempt to Enter Barracks

SPECIAL

CAMP BRECKINRIDGE, Ky. Six WAC'S quit the army this week, refusing to scrub floors

The girls, trained at Fort D Moines for army supply club protested when they were assigned to stacking beds and scrubbing floors in a warehouse.

Dissent increased until the final assignment came to wash painted walls in a laundry. Protest to Colonel Kelly proved unavailing. Then they went on a strike for five days.

The girls were allowed to resign under the new regulation which incorporates the former WAAC into the army as WAC.

WAC'S who resigned are Ruth M. Jones, daughter of the Rev. Russell C. Jeter, pastor of Tabernacle Baptist Church, Atlantic City, and Beatrice Brashear, Gladys Morton, Margaret Colemart, Mae E. Nichols, and Viola Bessups, all of New York.

The majority of the WAC'S who remained and are doing the scrubbing are Southern girls, Auxiliary Jones explained, and they were afraid to join the six who were discharged in protesting.

It's WAC Now

It is a Women's Army Corps now instead of Women's Auxiliary Army Corps. During the change over, any WAC not desiring to come under army discipline can return to civilian life.

A Disturbance

The War Department said on Tuesday it had received word about the Breckinridge incident and that there was foundation for the girls' complaint. "They were not given proper assignments," and there was a disturbance.

The Breckinridge public relations officer admitted the girls had resigned but refused details.

A New York girl at Breckinridge wrote her mother that white soldiers had sought to evade guards and enter their barracks at night. Officers protected them.

Asked what happened after the soldiers got inside, the WAC declined to state, adding that she understood letters were read and censored on the post.

The *Afro-American*, a weekly Baltimore newspaper, reports the U.S. War Department acknowledged black WAACs were improperly assigned to wash walls at Camp Breckinridge, Kentucky, July 10, 1943.

CHAPTER 6

Black Soldiers Get the Dirty Work

Camp Breckinridge, Kentucky, 1943

Ruth M. Jones, the daughter of a Baptist pastor in New Jersey, joined the army, trained as a supply clerk at Fort Des Moines, and was sent to Camp Breckinridge, Kentucky. Arriving at her assignment, Ruth was shocked when she was ordered to stack beds, scrub warehouse floors, and clean toilets.

You're in the South now, Colonel Clyde Parmelee told Ruth and other WAACs from the North. And in the South, he said, Negroes know their place.

Even women with college degrees were assigned grunt jobs. The women protested. They'd volunteered for the WAAC expecting their skills to make a difference in the war effort. Their objections were "rewarded" with orders to go wash walls in the laundry. Doing laundry was not an approved job for WAACs. At Breckinridge, civilians had done it. WAACs were meant to assume responsibilities that would release military men for combat.

No white WAACs on the post performed menial labor. Ruth and twenty other black WAACs decided they wouldn't either. They refused to report for duty, charging discrimination.

Colonel Parmelee warned them, "insubordination . . . is mutiny and next to murder, it is possibly the most serious [offense] in the service." Hearing they could be jailed or sentenced to hard labor with no pay, the black women reared in the South went back to work. But Ruth and five other northern women refused. They waited, wondering what punishment would come.

Coincidentally, at this time, July 1943, Congress disbanded the WAAC and allowed females to enlist, not as auxiliaries, but as actual members of the army. WAACs could transition to the new Women's Army Corps (WAC) or leave with an honorable discharge. The new WAC gave army women pay, privileges, and protection equal to men, but at Camp Breckinridge, it also gave the army an out. Ruth and the others who

refused to work in the laundry were allowed to resign with no penalty, which they did.

Another WAC, Zelda Webb, of Baltimore, Maryland, managed to get away with refusing orders at Camp Breckinridge when a different commander, Colonel R. C. Throckmorton, was in charge, possibly because she was an officer.

"In a pronounced southern accent he told me, 'You're going over to that WAC company, and you're going to be a mess officer.'

"'Sir, I have not had any mess training,' I said.

"'All you n— know how to cook,' he said.

"I said, 'You just met one who does not know how to cook; but if you send me to Fort Eustis, Virginia, for training I will come back and be the best mess officer you have on this post.'

"He said, 'I ain't sending you to no school, and you're going over there to be a mess officer.' When I about-faced, I kept on going. I didn't even salute him.

"He pointed at me, and when he did that I grabbed his finger and said, 'As long as you live, don't you ever point your finger in my face. I am an officer and a gentleman by the same act of Congress that commissioned you.'"

Few women in the army corps spoke to their superiors that way without getting court-martialed, and Zelda didn't know it then, but she would later suffer consequences for her actions.

Reports continued to surface about black WACs assigned to improper menial jobs, and through the war years WAC administrators made informal inspections to try to make sure women were given appropriate duties. A later inspection at Breckinridge found thirty black WACs working in the laundry, fifteen assigned to service jobs, including dishwashing at the base club, and five "well-educated Negro women . . . administration school graduates . . . employed sweeping warehouse floors."

It was the same across the South. At Fort Knox, Kentucky, black WACs worked in the kitchen. A white officer saying, "Most of these girls are much better off now than they were in civilian life."

In late 1942, General Dwight D. Eisenhower had requested typists and telephone operators to assist him in North Africa, and within two months of the first WAAC graduation, one hundred fifty white women were on their way across the Atlantic. White WAACs took up posts in Europe and Africa, working to help the war effort, while four hundred black WAACs waited for assignment at Fort Des Moines, marching in place. By mid-July 1943—one year after the WAAC was formed—the number of African American WAACs waiting for assignment at the Fort Des Moines Training Center neared nine hundred. Half lived in dayrooms due to lack of space in the barracks.

"The crowded living conditions, the scheduling of meals, and maintaining our high standards . . . plus the fact that these conditions existed because post commanders did not want Negro personnel, caused a morale problem," Captain Charity Adams said. "It was difficult to understand the logic that refused the use of trained personnel whose services can help end hostilities."

Some black women went outside official channels, contacting African American newspapers with their stories and writing War Department officials with their complaints. One letter writer made a direct appeal to President Roosevelt's wife, Eleanor. "I'm hoping you could fly down to Des Moines and look over the training camp and see this Negro, (one would perhaps find her scrubbing floors?) She holds the honor of Phi Beta and Sigma Chi and she has a [master's degree].

"You are so fine and so far above bigotry; I know you will do what you can for this dark skinned woman." There is no indication as to whether Eleanor Roosevelt responded to this letter.

There was often little WAC administrators could do to combat racist attitudes. WAC Chief Colonel Hobby sent Major Harriet West, a black WAC officer on her staff to visit army posts and convince white male commanders to employ black women. Some commanders reminded Major West that the WAC had been established to replace men for combat. Black

men were not allowed to carry guns and fight in the army, so these commanders didn't believe they had a responsibility to find suitable jobs for black women.

Several commanders said they could use hundreds of black women to work in laundry companies, but West told them WACs were only permitted to do jobs such as checking, sorting, and bundling clean clothes, not heavy manual labor in the laundry, which was usually contracted out to civilian workers. She did convince the commander of Fort Leonard Wood in Missouri to request one hundred fifty African American WACs for hospital work and as clerks and messengers. The commander at Fort Custer in Michigan agreed to requisition one hundred seventeen black women as typists.

In late 1944, as battlefields in Europe and the Pacific sent increasing numbers of wounded men back to the states, more hospitals opened to treat veterans, and there was increasing demand for WACs trained as medical and surgical technicians and laboratory aides. Recruiters made urgent appeals for women to join the army. A black newspaper, the *Oklahoma Eagle*, reported, "Gardiner General Hospital, one of the army's largest general hospitals" needs black WACs "as nurses' assistants."

Martha Putney got what she called the "choice assignment" of commanding fifty-five black WACs posted to work at Gardiner. When she arrived in Chicago, Martha was surprised to see the barracks where the women would live.

They were located in a public park next to the hospital where the federal government had leased land for the temporary barracks.

"It was newly constructed. It looked like a stockade, coiled wire on top of the ten-foot fence. It was [an] . . . area of scenic beauty. In fact, once we got out the gate you looked out there and you saw nothing but manicured lawn . . . then Lake Shore Drive . . . Lake Michigan not too far . . . less than a quarter mile away. It was beautiful out there."

The hospital commander, Colonel John R. Hall, told Martha the local lakeshore property owners association had protested African American WACs being posted to Gardiner because they feared it would decrease their property values. Whites in the exclusive Hyde Park neighborhood feared the black women might use the nearby whites-only beach.

"Now you're going to find out that I was one of them [against posting black

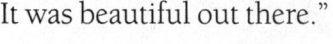
Chicago Defender, "WACs Perform Duties Despite Jim Crow Furore [*sic*]," July 7, 1945

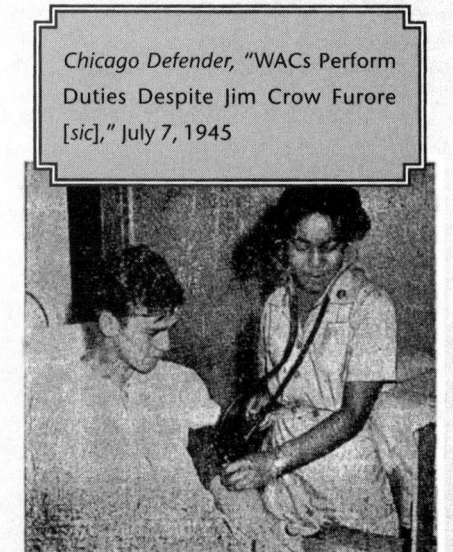

Although some of the white civilians in the neighborhood around Gardiner General hospital are up in arms over Negro WACs being stationed there, the white men who do the actual war chores don't seem to share their objections. Here, Pvt. Maxton Oliver of Woodsdale, N. C., watches as WAC Sgt. Werner K. Ertle of Chicago takes his blood pressure at the Hyde Park hospital.—Photos by Scott Tyler.

WACs at Gardiner], too," Colonel Hall told Martha, "But the War Department sent you here. It's my duty to accept you, tolerate you."

None of the white patients in the hospital objected to the black WACs taking their blood pressures or otherwise treating them. "In fact, they praised them," Martha said. "And before we left, the people who had complained and protested apologized in writing, and signed their names, and congratulated us for having done an efficient job."

Before the war's end, black women would serve at U.S. Army posts across the country from Fort Huachuca, Arizona, to Fort Dix, New Jersey, Fort Sam Houston, Texas, to Walla Walla, Washington, and spots in between like Fort Sheridan, Illinois, and Fort Knox, Kentucky. But as of February 1944, black WACs continued to experience crowded quarters at Fort Des Moines. ★

CHAPTER 7

Black WACs Strike for Fair Jobs

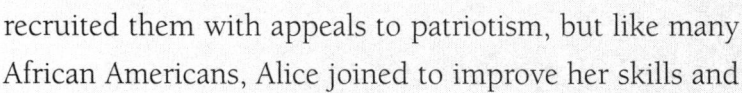

Fort Devens, Massachusetts, 1945

In civilian life, Alice E. Young, twenty-three, held a good-paying job at the U.S. Treasury Department. She dreamed of becoming a nurse and had completed a year of nursing school while working as a student in a Washington, D.C., hospital.

The WAC needed smart women like Alice and recruited them with appeals to patriotism, but like many African Americans, Alice joined to improve her skills and knowledge. The recruiting officer told her that with her education and experience she was qualified to be a WAC medical technician. Similar to a nurse, she would work with patients on a hospital ward.

After basic training, Alice was promised a spot in a medical technology school. While waiting for a spot to open, she was assigned to Lovell General Hospital at Fort Devens, Massachusetts. Her work included sitting with postoperative patients, taking temperatures, and checking blood pressures.

One day, the commander of the hospital, Colonel Walter Crandall, toured her ward. He saw Alice taking a white soldier's temperature and announced he'd have no "black WACs taking temperatures" in his hospital. "They are here to scrub and wash floors, wash dishes, and do all the dirty work," he said.

Alice was demoted to hospital orderly, her hopes of going to medical technology school dashed. She cleaned the hospital hallways and kitchen, washed dishes, cooked and served food, and took out the garbage. Sixty percent of the black WACs at Lovell had similar duties.

Only 7 percent of white WACs at Lovell were orderlies. Most of the white women worked as technicians in the laboratory, dispensaries, clinics, and on the wards. Alice said, "The uniforms were even changed. We had on blue, and they had complete white uniforms."

Many of the black WACs at Fort Devens believed duties were assigned unjustly. Private Miriam Doss felt the cleaning jobs she was assigned were beneath her dignity. "[I] never saw any white WACs cleaning floors. I didn't . . . join the army to wash windows. I could have stayed at home and been a maid."

The women protested their assignments through proper channels, but four months later they were still doing the same drudgery. Alice requested a transfer to the motor pool, but Colonel Crandall allegedly told her, "They want no blacks working at the motor pool."

The women finally became so distraught, they refused to report for work.

The *Chicago Defender* reported that one hundred "Negro WACs" staged a strike after the college-trained women were forced to scrub floors and wash windows, March 24, 1945.

DEVENS WACS STAGE SITDOWN

By EUGENE C. ZACK
(Defender Staff Correspondent)

FORT DEVENS, Mass.— Charging racial discrimination, 100 Negro WACs at this post staged a brief sitdown strike Saturday.

As the result of the strike at Lovell General hospital, brought about when college-trained Negro WACs who had enlisted as medical technicians had been forced to scrub floors and wash windows, disciplinary action has been taken against five members of the company.

Lieut.-Col. Walter A. Brown, chief of public relations for the First Service Command, made the following official statement concerning the brief strike:

"The Negro WAC medical company stationed at Lovell General hospital refused to report for duty Saturday. Disciplinary action was taken against five members of the company, after which the balance returned to duty."

Alice, Miriam, and a total of fifty-three black WACs staged a strike. One by one, throughout the day, higher- and higher-ranking white officers came and told the group the army would not tolerate soldiers refusing to do their duty, and that the penalty would be harsh. The women did not give in.

The following morning when the women had not returned to their posts, Major General Sherman Miles decided to put an end to the "mutiny." He arrived at the WAC barracks, assembled the black women, and—to make sure they

Article from the Baltimore, Maryland, *Afro-American* newspaper reporting on the sit-down strike of black WACs at Lovell General Hospital, Fort Devens, Massachusetts, March 17, 1945

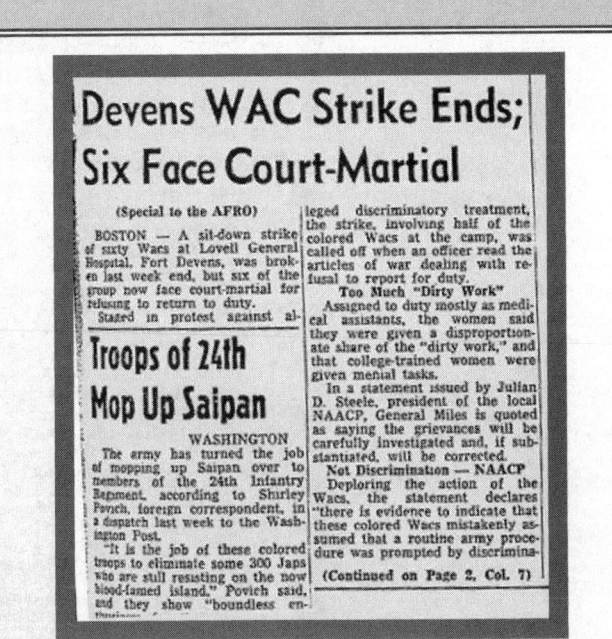

Devens WAC Strike Ends; Six Face Court-Martial

(Special to the AFRO)

BOSTON — A sit-down strike of sixty Wacs at Lovell General Hospital, Fort Devens, was broken last week end, but six of the group now face court-martial for refusing to return to duty. Staged in protest against al-

leged discriminatory treatment, the strike, involving half of the colored Wacs at the camp, was called off when an officer read the articles of war dealing with refusal to report for duty.

Too Much "Dirty Work"

Assigned to duty mostly as medical assistants, the women said they were given a disproportionate share of the "dirty work," and that college-trained women were given menial tasks.

In a statement issued by Julian D. Steele, president of the local NAACP, General Miles is quoted as saying the grievances will be carefully investigated and, if substantiated, will be corrected.

Not Discrimination — NAACP

Deploring the action of the Wacs, the statement declares "there is evidence to indicate that these colored Wacs mistakenly assumed that a routine army procedure was prompted by discrimina-

(Continued on Page 2, Col. 7)

Troops of 24th Mop Up Saipan

WASHINGTON

The army has turned the job of mopping up Saipan over to members of the 24th Infantry Regiment, according to Shirley Povich, foreign correspondent, in a dispatch last week to the Washington Post.

"It is the job of these colored troops to eliminate some 300 Japs who are still resisting on the now blood-famed island." Povich said, and they show "boundless en-

understood the situation—ordered Article of War No. 64 read aloud.

"Any person subject to military law . . . [who] willfully disobeys any lawful command of his superior officer, shall suffer death or such other punishment as a court-martial may direct."

"I now give each and every one of you the following direct order." General Miles said. He told them to go out, line up, and march to their duty posts and stay there. All of the women followed his orders.

But Alice was too upset to work, and after an hour she left her post on Ward 33 telling the ward master, "I will take a court-martial."

Another WAC, twenty-two-year-old Private Anna C. Morrison assigned to Ward 29, also decided to leave. "I was hysterical. I felt I could just lay down and die."

"If it will help my people by me taking a court-martial . . . put my name down," she said.

Private Mary E. Green, aged twenty, and Private Johnnie Murphy, twenty-one, also refused to work. "I would take death before I would go back to work," Johnnie Murphy said.

The four women were jailed and ordered to stand trial. A nine-member court-martial panel was convened to hear the case. It included two white WAC officers, two black army officers, and five white army officers. The four women

sat facing the panel and listened to their superior officers testify against them.

The trial lasted two days. The women were questioned and cross-examined in minute detail about what they had thought, said, and done after hearing General Miles' order.

The women's defense attorney, Julian D. Rainey, provided by the Boston chapter of the NAACP, argued the issue went deeper than disobeying orders. "They enlisted to see what they could do for their country. Then they found they were segregated because of an accident of birth. Where you find segregation, it is necessary to fight. Nobody can pat themselves on the back because they happened to be born white or yellow [sic], because it might have been otherwise.

"These women made this gesture of protest in hope that someday their descendants might enjoy fully the rights and liberties promised to Americans."

Extra!

Colonel Wh

Col. Walter M. Crandal
General Hospital, Fort Dev
making prejudicial remarks
installation, will be relieved

INSIDE THIS WEEK

How Wounded Vets Fare at U.S. Army Hospital.—Feature Page.

Why 366th Infantry Regiment Was Broken Up.—Page 11.

Photos of Consecration Ceremony for P.E. Bishop.—Page 10.

THE AF

53rd Year, No. 37

Contents of This Newspaper Copyrighted, 1945 by The AFRO-AMERICAN Company

BALTIMORE,

Alice testified that white WACs had easier duties at Lovell Hospital. "They do practically nothing, sir. They sit with patients, they read stories to them, help them write letters home . . . the work they do is altogether different."

The army prosecutor assured the court he was not seeking the death penalty, but said the women were guilty and should be punished.

After three days in jail and two days on trial, the four young women could hardly contain their emotional turmoil as they waited to hear the verdict. The court reached a decision in less than two hours. By secret ballot, two-thirds of the members voted all four women guilty as charged. They would go to prison.

News headline in the *Afro-American* heralds the removal of the U.S. Army colonel who had caused Fort Devens black WACs to strike, April 28, 1945

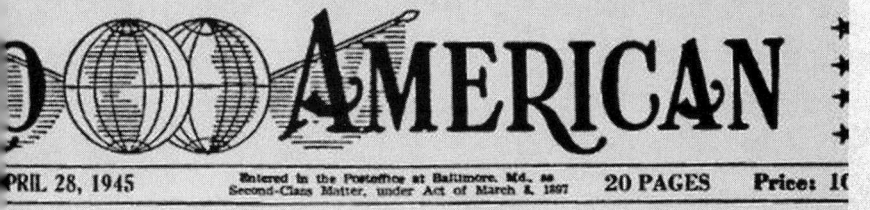

...aused Ft. Devens Wac Strike Removed

...manding officer of Lovell ...ass., who was accused of ...red Wacs assigned to that ...command, a War Depart-

ment source revealed Monday. At the request of the First Service Command, it was learned, Maj. Gen. Norman T. Kirk, the Surgeon General, has been asked to designate another
(Continued on Page 17, Column 7)

...AMERICAN

...PRIL 28, 1945   Entered in the Postoffice at Baltimore, Md., as Second-Class Matter, under Act of March 3, 1897   20 PAGES   Price: 10...

It was too much for Anna, she broke down weeping and had to be helped from the room by a friend. Alice, Mary, and Johnny bore the shock silently. The four were sentenced to military jail, where they would serve one year of hard labor before being dishonorably discharged from service.

People all over the country were upset over the severity of the sentences. Hundreds of people, white and black, protested in letters to army officials, the secretary of war, and President Roosevelt. Many argued that Colonel Crandall should be the one punished, for he'd failed to follow the army's separate but equal policy.

One white woman wrote, saying African Americans would have to wonder "why so many thousands of young men are giving their lives in a war to wipe out Nazism when there is mounting evidence of its flourishing at home."

Within weeks, the War Department reversed the verdict on a technicality, reinstated the women, and transferred them away from Fort Devens. The army did not investigate Colonel Crandall's behavior, but he was relieved of his hospital command and pressured to retire. Officers at Lovell Hospital were prohibited from assigning black WACs menial jobs like scrubbing floors. The courage of Alice, Anna, Mary, and Johnnie made a difference. ★

CHAPTER 8

Violence Targets Black WACs

All across America women rallied to the war effort, taking factory, office, and medical jobs, as well as joining the military. The country pulled together against a common threat. African American WACs had to stay vigilant for their personal safety in a way that whites did not. Even dressed in the uniform of their country they were not always safe.

"It's strange how you could feel the hate," said one woman. "That was something that I'd thought I'd gotten used to. All we wanted to do was work and serve."

WACs from Fort Des Moines alight from a train at Fort Huachuca, 1942.

That hate motivated violent attacks and death threats.

Terrorists threatened Charity Adams on a family visit to South Carolina. After attending a local meeting of the NAACP, she and her father came home to find the Ku Klux Klan waiting. Menacing figures in white robes, with hoods hiding their faces, sat in cars lining both sides of the street outside the Adamses' house.

The KKK spread fear throughout the southern states by regularly lynching blacks on the slightest provocation. In the 1930s and '40s, people were rarely prosecuted and even more rarely convicted for these killings. Their presence evoked terror throughout black neighborhoods. But Charity and her father showed no fear, walking tall between the cars, down the street, and into their home.

"Daddy got out his double-barreled shotgun and shells, gave instructions to Mamma, my younger sister and brother and me . . . we could see the men clearly . . . could peep through the slats of the venetian blinds and would occasionally see one of the men light a cigarette."

They called the police, but the white police force "couldn't do anything about men parked on the street." Afraid to sleep, Charity stood vigil as the KKK persisted in their intimidation until dawn.

Charity was lucky she only endured threats, resentment, and verbal abuse. But other African American WACs suffered physical attacks. One Negro WAC officer was beaten,

Charity said, because "of anger a 'n—' could be a captain and expect white people to salute her."

There are dozens of stories of African American WACs mistreated while riding buses and trains. Their U.S. military uniforms provoked hostility from civilians, and at southern posts WACs felt they risked their lives simply by leaving army grounds.

On December 23, 1944, white policemen in Gadsden, Alabama, beat and arrested two black WACs after they refused to give up their seats to whites. Private Gladys Blackman and Private Roberta McKenzie were sitting in seats designated for blacks in the rear of the bus. As the bus filled with white people, the driver ordered them to stand and surrender their

A report from the *Amsterdam Star News* on the case of two black WACs beaten and arrested by Gadsden, Alabama, police after refusing to give up their seats to whites, December 1944.

N. Y. WAC BEATEN BY DIXIE COP

THE AMSTERDAM-STAR NEWS
New York City

She Now Faces Court Martial, Letter Avers

Girl Is Called 'Winch?'
'Smart Northerner,' By
Policeman In Kentucky

By CONSTANCE CURTIS

Following an unmerciful beating by a civilian policeman in Elizabethtown, Ky., because she dared sit in a waiting room reserved for white people, a WAC private faces summary court martial this Saturday for breaking the Jim Crow laws of the state. The woman, Pfc. Helen Smith of Syracuse, who has served 26 months in the Corps and is now stationed at Fort Knox, lay ill in the hospital for a full week before she was able to write of her plight to relatives here and in Philadelphia.

Two years before her beating by police, WAAC Georgia Boson (*second from left*) is shown receiving supplies with other women of the 35th detachment, Fort Knox, Kentucky, 1943.

seats to white passengers. When the women stayed seated, he refused to start the bus. A passenger stepped off and called local police.

A cop arrived and dragged one of the WACs from her seat. The other WAC pushed the policeman and demanded he call military police (MP), as he had no authority to put his hands on military personnel. He did not call an MP and arrested the black women. As he dragged them from the bus, white passengers—women and men—shouted "kill 'em, kill 'em."

A newspaper reported the two women were forced into a squad car where police continued to beat Private Gladys Blackman. When they arrived at the jail, the cop pounded her head against the wall until she was only semiconscious. When military authorities arrived to pick up the women, both had been beaten. Gladys was injured so badly she had to spend a week in bed.

In July 1945, Private First Class Helen Smith of Syracuse, New York, was catching a Greyhound bus in Elizabethtown, Kentucky. Seeing no empty seats in the colored waiting room, she sat on a bench close by. Black WACs Tommie Smith and Private Georgia Boson had joined her when a police officer started shouting at them.

"Git up and git out of here. This place ain't for n——s, this place is for white people."

The WACs asked him to call MPs, but the cop clobbered Georgia over the head with his blackjack, yelling, "When we

The Baltimore, Maryland, *Afro-American* newspaper reports WACs Georgia Boson and Helen Smith face court-martial after being assaulted by Kentucky cop, July 28, 1945.

tell n—s to move, we mean for them to git."

Private Tommie Smith ran to find an MP. Helen begged bystanders to help, but "they never moved." She tried to help Georgia, and the policeman turned on her. He whacked Helen on the head and dragged her across the floor of the station. He and another cop hauled the three women to the city jail.

When MPs came, not to help the WACs, but to take them into custody, Helen was still bleeding. She had a swollen face, two black eyes, and a tooth knocked loose. When they got to Fort Knox, the post commander ignored

---

Afro-American (Negro)
Baltimore, Md.
134
DATE: JUL 28 1945

2 Wacs Slugged by Kentucky Cop

Pair Had Refused to Move in Bus Station

FACE COURT-MARTIAL

Officer Upheld by Fort Knox Commander

PHILADELPHIA

How she and another Wac were blackjacked in a Louisville, Ky., bus station by a civilian policeman was described by Pfc. Helen Smith, former Philadelphian, in a letter to her sister, Mrs. Catherine McCabe of 2201 Ellsworth St.

Stationed at Fort Knox, both Pfc. Smith, wife of a World War I veteran and mother of a son serving overseas in the Army, and her companion, Pvt. Georgia Bosum, face court-martial proceedings as a result of the incident.

Originally charged with violating the State jim crow laws and assaulting a civilian officer, the two were later charged with violating the 93rd Article of War; i.e., being disorderly in uniform.

Kentucky does not have any law which requires segregation in train or bus stations.

According to the letter, the two Wacs were sitting in the section of the bus station reserved for whites when they were approached by the policeman and ordered to get out.

Told that the section reserved for colored was overcrowded and that they were simply waiting for a bus, the cop retorted, "When white people down here tell n - - -s to move they move," the letter said.

Threatening to place them under arrest, he continued to use offensive epithets and when Private Bosum protested he hit her over the head with his blackjack, Pfc. Smith wrote:

Left Bleeding

When she came to her companion's rescue, the cop slugged her severely with his weapon, leaving her battered and bloody, she continued.

When the pair were returned to camp, the post commander ignored their plight and lectured to them on obeying jim crow laws in the South, she informed her sister further. The NAACP has been asked to investigate the incident.

Helen's need for medical attention and reprimanded the three women for not obeying Jim Crow, the laws that enforced racial segregation in the southern states.

When Helen finally got to the hospital for treatment, her tooth was so damaged it had to be pulled. It was days before she felt well enough to write a letter to family in New York. "I guess you wondered why you did not hear from me last week . . . The things that have happened to me are like a horrible dream, except they happened and are very real."

Fort Knox commander Colonel R. C. Throckmorton criminally charged the three WACs, alleging they had attacked the policemen and disobeyed segregation laws. The NAACP rushed an attorney to Elizabethtown, who argued that the State of Kentucky, in fact, did not have laws on the books requiring segregation of bus stations or public buildings. The attorney managed to get the assault charges lessened to disorderly conduct.

At the women's court-martial trial, the army prosecutor called the two policemen and several of the town residents to testify against Helen, Georgia, and Tommie, but in the end the panel found the women innocent.

Black newspapers accused Colonel Throckmorton of failing to protect U.S. personnel, and putting a "stamp of approval on the acts of prejudiced southerners." Editorials demanded the army take action against Colonel Throckmorton and the Elizabethtown police. The army did neither.

In a case less conspicuous, but just as menacing, WAC Elsie Oliver was sent to a Fort Des Moines army dentist, rumored to be racist. One by one, white patients came and went until near dark, when the assistant finally called Elsie's name.

Sitting in the dental chair, she noticed the instruments were dirty. "Sir, you're not going to work on me with that!" Elsie said.

"'I am the dentist, you'll do as I tell you' . . . He pushed my head back and started pawing in my mouth." After the dental treatment Elsie's mouth became so severely infected, she was hospitalized for nearly a month.

Black WACs best recourse was often to go outside military channels with their difficulties and contact African American newspapers like the *Chicago Defender* and the *Pittsburgh Courier* or well-known activist Dr. Mary McLeod Bethune. A number of African American women quit the army as soon as their time was up or went absent without leave (AWOL). But most endured and tried to serve as best they could.

WAC Ardell Gripes left Fort Jackson, South Carolina, on a one-day pass, and couldn't get back. "Each time I went to the bus station, the driver told me there was no more room for colored passengers," she said. For five days, Ardell tried and failed to return to Fort Jackson. When she finally made it, she was punished for being AWOL. "I was made to write three letters [of explanation] and was given three days garbage detail as a result of my being AWOL."

Edna Edmonson Brown had train conductors and taxi drivers in New Orleans refuse to let her ride and had trouble with civilians both on and off post in Mississippi. "The WAAC was an unknown world, but I'm glad I was brave enough to accept the challenge," she said. ★

CHAPTER 9

Called for Overseas Duty

Fort Oglethorpe, Georgia, to Birmingham, England, 1945
As the war raged a second year, a third, and into a fourth, African American WACs felt one particular symptom of racial bias at every post and all ranks. White WACs had been sent to Europe in 1942 and the army's refusal to send black WAC units for duty overseas was a nagging, painful discouragement.

African American newspapers and civic leaders pressed the issue. But even as the army desperately needed clerical

Women's Army Corps Private First Class Alyce Dixon (*right*) talks with a superior officer while serving with the 6888th Postal Battalion, 1945.

workers in Europe to relieve male soldiers for combat, and hundreds of capable black women sat unassigned at Fort Des Moines, the answer was always no. Black WACs would not be sent overseas.

The War Department deflected blame: "WAC units are shipped overseas in answer to specific requests from theater commanders. No Negro WAC units have been requested to date."

But in late 1944, the army was short postal workers to sort mail for troops fighting in Europe. A huge backlog of mail was stored in Birmingham, England. Army leaders decided that sending a large number of black WACs far away from the American South and distant from the bulk of U.S. forces would not likely inflame racial tension.

Early on, Charity Adams had given up any hope she'd be sent overseas. She had no idea why she was summoned to her boss's office in December 1944. He astonished her by asking if she'd like to lead a battalion to Europe. Battalion commanders usually held the rank of colonel, but Charity had only been promoted from captain to major. She'd seen white captains and majors promoted more quickly than her but tried not to let that get her down. If she went to Europe, she'd remain a major but carry the responsibility of commanding a battalion. She agreed to go.

"The truth was, I had been involved in so many firsts I did not want to be left out of any new venture." That venture

As part of their training for overseas service, WACs climb down a cargo net at Fort Des Moines.

Gladys (Schuster) Carter, 6888th Central Postal Directory Battalion, 1945

proved to be Charity's biggest challenge yet as a black officer in the WAC.

The overseas training for the 6888th Central Postal Directory Battalion would be at Fort Oglethorpe, Georgia, and nearly one thousand black WACs started to arrive from posts across the country. They had the option to decline the appointment to Europe with the 6888th Postal Battalion, but most were enthusiastic.

"I think I would have climbed a mountain to get on the list [to go]," Private First Class Gladys Schuster Carter said. "We were going to do our duty. Despite all the bad things that happened in the country, this was our home. This is where I was born."

Corporal Virginia Lane Frazier was only nineteen and eager for adventure. "Who would have ever thought that a little girl

from Minnesota, black at that, would go away to Europe? It was very exciting."

Private First Class Elsie Oliver of Burkeville, Virginia, went so far as to phone Eleanor Roosevelt to make sure she didn't miss the opportunity to go overseas. She was stationed at Camp Gruber, Oklahoma, as a cook, and she must have been a good one because her company commander didn't want her to leave.

"She told me that she was going to delete my name from the list," Elsie said. "I went to the supreme commander of the whole post, Colonel Lockett. He was over everybody, both white and black. He knew me because he ate at our mess hall."

The commander suggested she talk with Eleanor Roosevelt. In a move that would most likely never happen now in twenty-first-century America, he told Elsie, "Here's my telephone."

She put in a call to President Roosevelt's wife and was told she was in a meeting. Elsie left a message.

"Colonel Lockett took me back down to my WAC detachment . . . and the phone rang and it was Mrs. Roosevelt. She asked my company officer, 'Do you know Elsie Oliver? Have her ready for shipment at four p.m. today.'" Elsie was the first one waiting for the train that afternoon, headed for Fort Oglethorpe and overseas training.

Zelda Webb, the WAC who had shaken her finger at Colonel Throckmorton earlier, and refused to report to work in the mess, heard from friends that her name was on the list

to go overseas, but her orders never came. "Finally I went to Colonel Throckmorton," she said. "He tells me the real truth. 'We had your name taken off of the list to go overseas.'" He was punishing her for her earlier insubordination.

Zelda was glad to know why she wasn't going overseas. She did not regret speaking out to the colonel. "If I had succumbed to the treatment that they had given other blacks before, or not spoken up for myself, my morale would have been down, and I would have been doing work that I did not like," she said. "You can't go around shuffling your feet with your head hung down acting apologetic. If you see something you want, you must go after it. One day somebody will recognize it, and it's a victory for you, especially when it's somebody who has denigrated you because of your race."

Once training got under way for the 6888th at Fort Oglethorpe, Charity went ahead to Europe to organize accommodations for her troops, learn about the job they would do, and prepare for the women to start work as soon as they arrived.

Reporting for duty in London, Charity discovered she'd not only be dodging German bombs in the streets but continuing to face the home front enemy, too. Some U.S. military men had trouble accepting black officers. Accepting black *women* officers? Unimaginable.

"Salutes were slow in coming, and frequently, returned with great reluctance," Charity said.

But the city was filled with military people from the Allied and neutral countries around the world. In the streets, Charity felt her minority status disappear. "Every conceivable kind of uniform could be seen on the streets, worn by all races, colors, shapes, sizes, sexes, and religious persuasions. As we stared at the uniforms and the people, they stared at us."

Charity quickly learned to carry on like a Londoner. "It was safe as long as we could hear the motor in the bomb, for that meant that it was still moving across England; it was only when the motor stopped that we held our breath, knowing the bomb was on its way down. Only when we heard the explosion, or enough time had passed did we exhale."

A scene of devastation following a V2 rocket attack, somewhere in the south of England. Civil defense workers search through debris and rubble, checking for any other survivors, 1945.

Soon Charity left the bombs of London behind and went north to Birmingham to get ready for her troops.

Back in the states, the women selected for the 6888th trained for the war. Private Mary McBride had left a professional dance career to join the WAC. Now in the army, she crawled on her belly under barbed wire, bullets flying overhead. "They say if you raise up, they'll kill you. They scare you half to death. I don't know whether it was live ammunition, but you had to learn how to do that stuff to save your life."

Private Mary Crawford Ragland was right out of high school in Wilmington, Delaware, when she saw an army recruiting advertisement offering black women a chance to go overseas. She enlisted at seventeen. Soon she regretted it because the training was so hard. "I wanted to go home," Mary said, laughing about it later. "But I didn't want to go to jail, so I stayed."

WAC Dorothea Gee Bartlett had worked as a silk finisher in the New York City garment district. Now she climbed ropes and cargo nets. "We had a mock ship, and we had to learn how to get up and come down," Dorothea said. "Some of the girls froze, and some of the sergeants had to go up and get them."

Perhaps more frightening, the women learned what to say and how to act if they were captured by the enemy. They needed to recognize enemy aircraft, ships, and weapons. "We were trained how to detect gas bombs and gas attacks," Corporal Myrtle Rhoden said. "We were trained how to disperse

Col. Hobby chats with enlisted women at Camp Shanks, N. Y., before contingent sailed for England. Unit was first group of Negro WACs given overseas assignment.

Negro WAC Unit Sent Overseas

Train speeds WACs to New York Port of Embarkation and start of great adventure. Women, most of whom asked overseas assignment, were given extensive training.

The *Sunday Mirror* reports Colonel Hobby visits the 6888th at Camp Shanks, New York, before they embark for England. Black WACs on a train to Port of New York where they will set sail for duty in Europe, February 18, 1945.

over to the side of the road and to go down in the ditch . . . that type of warfare training."

In early February 1945, the women of the 6888th took the train from Georgia to Camp Shanks in New York, ready to ship overseas. No doubt they remembered the words Charity had spoken to them on their very first day of training for this overseas assignment. "The eyes of the world" were upon them.

Captain Abbie Noel Campbell, the 6888th's second in command to Major Adams, said, "We could either do a good job and receive praise or do a bad job and receive ridicule." ★

A crowd of African American Women's Army Corps members waving at the camera. Staten Island Terminal, New York Port of Embarkation, February 1945.

CHAPTER 10

The 6888th Goes to Europe

February 1945

The first of two contingents of the 6888th boarded the *Ile de France*, a former luxury liner. They sailed from New York City, Myrtle Rhoden's hometown—five hundred women and thousands of male U.S. military personnel. The women were given staterooms on the top deck. "It was loaded to the brim," Myrtle said, "with troops and equipment and bombs and ammunition and whatever else was needed for war."

Corporal Ruth E. Jefferson had grown up in a small town. Joining the WAC had opened a entirely new world for her, but crossing the Atlantic was not a high point. "All I remember is that I was sick the whole time," she said.

Private First Class Gladys O. Thomas, a fun-loving, athletic young woman, was one of the lucky ones who didn't get seasick. When storms in the North Atlantic rocked the ship with heavy waves, she enjoyed it. One night the erratic motion was so strong it woke Gladys. Someone told her a German submarine was chasing the ship and firing torpedoes. She didn't believe it. She turned over and went back to sleep.

The 6888th Central Postal Directory Battalion arriving in England, February 1945

But it was true. The ship zigzagged to avoid the torpedoes. Myrtle was wide-awake. "It lasted, they tell me, forty-five minutes; but honestly I thought it was much longer. You had to hang on with all your strength because the veering was so severe—the pulling and turning. I could hear the noise outside: the sirens, the banging, the horns and whistles . . . Lots of screaming. I thought, this is the end. I really did. I said my prayers. One or two girls were crying in my squadron. And finally it ended. It just stopped."

Corporal Essie Dell O'Bryant Woods, from Augusta, Georgia, had joined the army with her two sisters and she knew

her mother worried about them. "The strange thing about being in danger, you are not afraid," Essie said. "And you don't realize how dangerous it was until after it's over. We were lucky, I guess, lucky."

The *Ile de France* delivered the first contingent of the 6888th safely to Glasgow, Scotland, and they boarded the train for England. In all, eight hundred eighty African American WACs were assigned to the 6888th in Birmingham. The second group of women would arrive about two months later, their journey uneventful.

Corporal Lucia Pitts, who had been stationed at Fort Huachuca in the Arizona desert, said she would never forget her first impression of the English countryside from the train.

"The farmlands looked lush and green, but at intervals there was snow. Everything was laid out so neatly and precisely, with trim hedgerows separating the plots, and little splashing falls here and there; and the land looked so clean it seemed it had been swept by a broom."

Darkness had fallen by the time they arrived at their new quarters at King Edward's School. They were pleased to find double-decker army bunks had been made up for them at the former boys' school, but the showers were a much less welcome sight. They were outside in a courtyard between buildings, and they had no shower curtains.

"It was cold and we took our showers as quickly as we could and went to bed," said Myrtle. "I remember that in the

following days I bathed by my bed out of my helmet most of the time."

The next morning, it was clear King Edward's School had seen the ravages of war. Over the next few weeks, the women would clean the buildings and patch holes in the roof.

"I had never been in a more depressing place in my life," said Captain Abbie Noel Campbell. "The corridors were narrow and dark. The rooms were small, ill-lighted, and poorly ventilated."

Charity Adams faced an immediate test. While the 6888th had been en route, she had been called to meet with the upper echelon of the communications network that included the mail sorting operation. Dinner with high-ranking officers could be nerve-wracking, and more so for African American women who came from states where segregation barred them from even sitting at a table with a white man.

"With all the 'spit and polish' we could muster, we tried to relax and be socially proper as well as act according to military courtesy," Charity said. Everything went smoothly until partway through the meal, the commanding general, Lieutenant General John C. H. Lee, put Charity on the spot. He turned to her and asked, "Adams, can your troops march?"

"There was only one answer to that," Charity said. "So my reply was, 'Yes, sir, they are the best marching troops you will ever see.'" As the words came out of her mouth, she realized, "I either had to prove my words or eat them later."

Charity knew army officers were judged on how well their troops performed in everything they did, even simply marching across a field. If a single soldier were out of step, or her uniform sloppy, it would reflect poorly on Charity's leadership skills. Just three days after the women landed in Glasgow, General Lee would come to inspect the battalion. Charity had to get five hundred travel-tired women in perfect marching order.

Once the women settled into quarters in Birmingham, Charity gave the orders and the women got ready: every shoe polished, every uniform wrinkle free and fitting properly, and hopefully, every woman recovered from seasickness. They practiced marching and at the appointed hour lined up at attention, waiting for General Lee. A large crowd of Birmingham citizens waited too, curious to see the newcomers.

"Ten minutes before the designated hour, I began to think the general was not coming," Charity said. "At one minute before the hour, General Lee and his entourage arrived. He was on time; [we were] early."

Charity gave the command. *Forward march*.

The 6888th U.S. Postal Battalion moved out, every foot in step, every arm swinging in time, every head and shoulder at the proper angle. The women knew they would have to work together to succeed in this mission. Plenty of people expected them to fail. The African American WACs represented not individuals, not simply their military unit, nor their country.

Major Charity Adams exchanges salute with Lieutenant General John C. H. Lee. Birmingham, England, February 15, 1945.

They represented every black person in America, and they were determined to prove themselves.

The 6888th Postal Directory Battalion passed inspection, crossing its first hurdle without flaw, and Charity breathed a sigh of relief. She was proud of her soldiers. But now they faced the overwhelming backlog of letters and packages that had to be sorted and redirected to soldiers all over the European Theater of Operations (ETO).

"We were just stymied by the mail stacked all over," Corporal Virginia Lane Frazier said. And more continued to arrive.

"Some Americans didn't understand about addressing letters, so they would just write a letter to their son or husband addressed 'To Junior, U.S. Army,' or 'To Sam, Army,'"

Mary Crawford Ragland said. "It was our job to figure out who those soldiers were and get them their mail." Sometimes return addresses were clues or information inside the letter. Some were undeliverable.

Besides redirecting the backed-up letters and packages, women worked censoring outgoing mail. All mili-

tary personnel knew they were not allowed to reveal troop locations or movements, and most did not. But outgoing mail had to be checked for sensitive information in case it fell into enemy hands. Censors blacked out any information that might be harmful to the Allied war effort.

The 6888th Postal Battalion on parade. Birmingham, England, February 15, 1945

Plowing through stacks of mail, the women felt connected to the soldiers they served. "There was part of the history of these men on the files," Private First Class Dorothy Turner said. "You could see the last time that this man got mail . . . you had this pile of mail that he should have gotten over the years . . . You knew that he had not gotten any news from his family or friends . . . and you were determined to try to find him."

It was difficult for the women when they received word that particular men on their rosters would never read the letters intended for them. "The wives and sweethearts would write every day," Corporal Alyce Dixon said, "so we had stacks of mail to send back—deceased."

U.S. troops almost buried by parcels do their best to handle the year's holiday mail, 1944.

A member of the 6888th Central Postal Directory Battalion sorts mail in Birmingham, England, 1945

Members of the all-black 6888th Postal Directory Battalion sorting and readdressing mail to American military personnel in Europe. Birmingham, England, 1945

Charity formed a unit focused on putting together broken and damaged packages. "They could take a box . . . look at the color of the paper, the indentation of the cans, and sometimes using the newspaper that was stuffed in the package, they could see where the package came from," Charity said. "I was just amazed at how good they were."

The women wore water-repellent clothes and boots to protect themselves from rotting cookies and nesting mice, as they repacked all that could be salvaged—jewelry, socks, or anything wearable—and sent it on to the soldiers.

Charity divided the 6888th into three eight-hour shifts, working around the clock, seven days a week to clear out the backlog of mail. Women worked in tight quarters and tried to adjust to the constant rotating schedule. "One week you had the morning shift and you would have to adjust to sleeping. When you had almost adjusted, then you'd have to go to another shift, and that was a hard thing to do; but we managed," Gladys Thomas Anderson said.

When the steam heating system wasn't working properly, the women worked in their field jackets and ski pants to stay warm. When their eyes grew strained from reading addresses in poorly lit work areas, they reminded themselves, *no mail, low morale*. They were doing important work. They were sending comfort, encouragement, and news from home to the soldiers fighting the Nazis.　　　　　★

CHAPTER 11

Welcomed as Equals

Birmingham, England, 1945

In Birmingham the African American women did not have to think about which water fountain to drink from. They did not have to worry about sitting in the wrong waiting room or looking at a white person too directly. And they didn't fear assault by the local police. In fact, many locals in Birmingham were eager to make friends with them and invited WACs into their homes for tea and made them welcome around town.

The Birmingham *Sunday Mercury* published an article about the African American visitors. "They have lively minds and an interest in historical England which is insatiable. They seem to know a great deal more about Shakespeare country than most Midlanders [residents of the area where Birmingham is located].

"These WACs are very different from the colored women portrayed on the films, where they are usually either domestics or the outspoken old-retainer type or sloe-eyed sirens given to gaudiness of costume and eccentricity in dress. The WACs have dignity and proper reserve."

One black WAC said. "At Fort Oglethorpe, we were just plain scared to even venture off the post, but in England we were treated like kings and queens."

Interracial marriage was legal in Britain, unlike in the United States, and some of the black WACs accepted dates with British men, though none developed into serious romantic relationships. Mostly, members of the 6888th enjoyed social activities that included British men in groups rather than couples.

Many members of the 6888th returned home with fond memories of the dignity and respect they experienced in England and later in France. They were not only entertained in public places like museums, ski resorts, theaters, restaurants, and pubs, many women were also welcomed and entertained

in private homes. "There were always invitations and parties to attend," said Myrtle Rhoden.

Racism did exist in Europe, but members of the 6888th encountered it mostly among Americans. Myrtle Rhoden recalled being treated badly by white American servicemen in a pub. "[The white soldiers] started verbally abusing [us] and declaring how dark the room had gotten as a result of us walking in. British men came to our side and rescued us and sat down. They told the American servicemen that they were out of place at which point the American soldiers got belligerent and were thrown out."

While traveling, Virginia Lane Frazier and two white WACs arrived in Bath, England, about ten at night, where the group was supposed to stay at American Red Cross accommodations. Virginia was turned away because she was black and luckily rescued by locals. "This wonderful English family took me in . . . It was beautiful."

The American Red Cross was involved in another incident of discrimination. The organization provided a hotel in London where WACs could stay when on leave from duty. Black and white women stayed there together until the Red Cross director announced a newly renovated hotel for black WACs.

"We realize that your colored girls would be happier if they had a hotel all to themselves," she told Charity.

Harriet M. West became the first black major in the U.S. Women's Army Corps on August 21, 1943. She served as an aide to WAC director, Oveta Culp Hobby, and as an adviser to the army on racial issues. West and Major Charity Adams were the only black women to attain the rank of major during World War II.

Charity disagreed. She called a meeting of her troops to explain the situation. She told them the segregated hotel was quite nice but asked them to stay elsewhere if they were in London overnight. To her knowledge, none of the eight hundred women ever used the hotel designated for them.

Sorting and redirecting mail continued day and night. Each shift, the WACs handled some sixty-five thousand letters and packages. They felt great satisfaction as the stacks of mail dwindled. "But more important," Margaret Y. Jackson said, "we [heard from] servicemen . . . profusely thanking us for the packets of mail and packages that they had been expecting for weeks or months but had received only after our arrival."

Morale in the 6888th was high. Segregated by race and gender, the battalion had full responsibility for managing its affairs and carrying out its mission. All the commissioned and noncommissioned officers were black women, filling roles of authority African American women had never held before. They led by example without heavy-handed control, earning the respect of the battalion. The lower-ranking women saw their officers as pioneers.

"We had some very strong black officers who were interested in our maintaining our sense of self and pride and race," Margaret said.

Major Charity Adams had been selected to lead the battalion based on her military leadership and technical skills, but she was also a charismatic woman who cared deeply about

the women she commanded. The black WACs respected her for her educational accomplishments, a college degree in mathematics, physics, and Latin and a minor in history, and for military rank. She was one of only two black WACs promoted to the rank of major.

"She was liked. Everybody admired her for who she was." Virginia Lane Frazier said. Private First Class Willie Whiting said, "She had brains and beauty. She had it all."

An example of Charity's concern for the personnel needs of her soldiers is the effort she made to requisition equipment for a beauty salon for the 6888th. "Even before leaving Fort Oglethorpe," Charity said, "the officers and I had discussed the need for beauty parlor equipment. How in the world could we keep morale up if the women did not feel that they could look their best?"

This wasn't something the army normally provided for women, though all forts offered barbershops for men. Back in the states, women could find services they needed in cities or towns near their duty stations, but in Europe, the hair treatment and colors of makeup needed by African American women were nonexistent. Charity was able to requisition beauty salon chairs for the 6888th, as well as straightening combs, Marcel irons, and special gas burners.

Word got around over the entire ETO that in Birmingham African American women could get their hair done "just like

back home," and the battalion beauty salon was besieged by black nurses and Red Cross workers who desperately wanted their hair fixed. "Members of our unit came first, but we tried to accommodate all comers," Charity said. "We were certain that no other army outfit in Europe had the kind of recreational equipment we had."

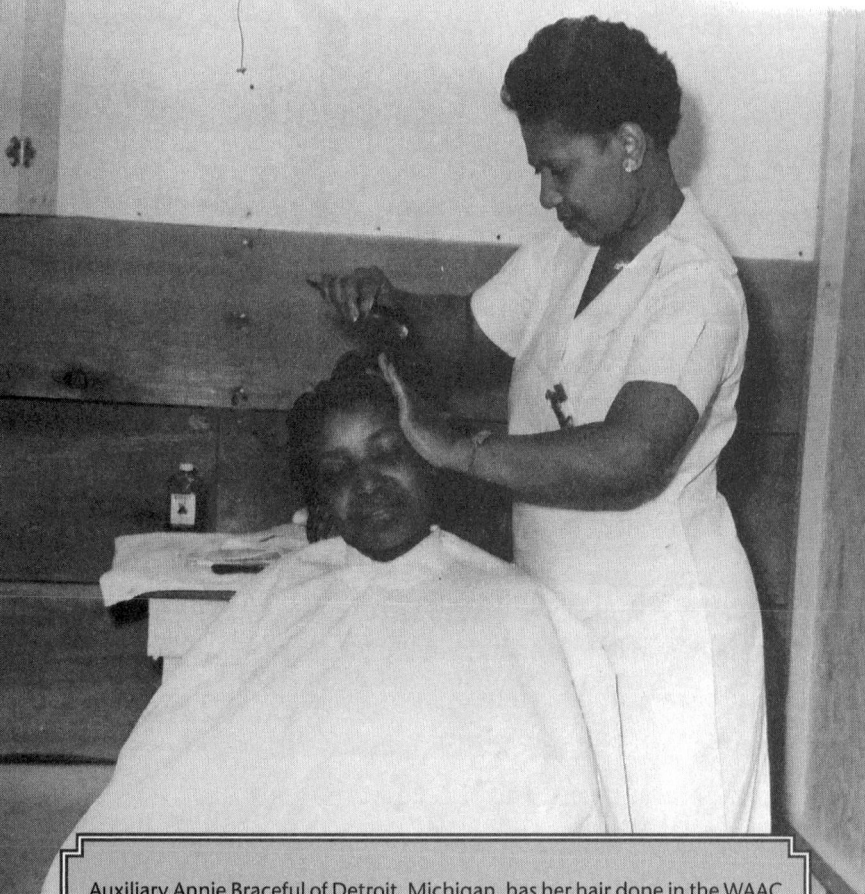

Auxiliary Annie Braceful of Detroit, Michigan, has her hair done in the WAAC beauty parlor attached to their post exchange (PX) and recreation hall. The operator is Miss Ethel Ware of Washington, D.C.

The battalion of eight hundred eighty women had been selected to include diverse backgrounds and civilian work experience including everything from clerks to hairdressers. This enabled the 6888th to function as a fully self-contained unit. Women assigned to Special Services had the job of keeping up morale, which included recreation and entertainment. Before enlisting in the army, Captain Mildred Carter had been a professional dancer, performed in Broadway musicals, and operated her own dance school. She was appointed Special Services Officer of the 6888th and organized an entertainment troupe that traveled to perform in hospitals and military installations throughout Europe.

Women also competed in sports including Ping-Pong, softball, volleyball, and basketball, and in their free time the women could travel. "Anyone who wanted to sign up could go on tours," said Corporal Mary Daniels Williams. "We went to London and we visited the countryside to look around old castles. We went through Windsor Castle, which is the place where the king and queen live when they're not in Buckingham Palace." These activities helped relieve the day-to-day stress of the job and built team spirit.

Corporal Gertrude Cruse Lavigne and other members of the 6888th basketball team qualified to compete for an all-star team composed of WAC players from throughout England. They were angry and disappointed when they were told they would not be allowed to play for the team because U.S. Army

WACs perform a musical number.

Private First Class Dorothy Ellis of Chicago reaches for a high ball in the 6888th team's softball practice. She played short center on the team, which won the championship for Chanor Base Section, northern France, and competed in the European Theater championships contest in the U.S. Riviera Recreational Area, Nice, France, 1945.

policy forbade racially mixed teams. They were allowed, however, to compete against the white WAC teams, and the all-star ban powered their efforts to play their best and win as many games as possible.

But whether at work or at play, it was wartime, and that reality was never far from the minds of the women. The windows of their workrooms and quarters were blacked out to hide their location from enemy planes, and the sound of air raid sirens was familiar to all. King Edward's School was never a target, but an army engineer unit of black men stationed forty miles away was almost totally destroyed in a bombing raid, and the men killed.

"That incident really brought it home to me," Private First Class Dorothy Dailey said. "These were actual human beings, some whom I had met. We were vulnerable like everybody else when the sirens went off." Dorothy also lost an English friend. "I had visited her and her family a couple of times and was scheduled to visit them this particular weekend. So I went to their house and nobody was there. The entire block had been demolished [by bombs] and I never heard from her again."

As the African American women settled into their work routine and experienced life without Jim Crow, they enjoyed a new vision of themselves. WAC Bertha Solomon Walker said, "We realized that we had self-worth, a right to be proud and dignified." ★

Members of the 6888th Central Postal Directory Battalion participate in a V-E Day parade. Birmingham, England, May 13, 1945.

CHAPTER 12

A Challenge to Leadership

Birmingham, England, 1945

The all-black WAC battalion was a curiosity for many American military personnel in Britain, and the unit was visited, congratulated, supervised, and reviewed by every officer of rank who could come up with an excuse to travel to Birmingham. That was besides official field inspections that were a normal part of army life. Charity Adams kept her troops in top form so they could work efficiently and in readiness for when her superior officers arrived to inspect the battalion.

The 6888th had had a month of good progress reducing the mounds of mail, and then in late March 1945, Charity received word to expect a commanding general to arrive and inspect her troops and their work. When she told this story later, she never named the man, but he was in her direct chain of command and his inspection would affect the reputation of the entire battalion. The white general arrived and examined the women's quarters and work areas. After lunch, the off-duty women lined up in formation for his review.

"Adams, where are the other personnel of this unit?" the general barked. "It certainly does not look like a battalion to me."

"Yes, sir," Charity answered, standing at attention. "We work eight-hour shifts, so some of the women are working." She explained another third of the battalion were sleeping.

"I wanted to review your troops. That means all of them," he said.

"But, sir—"

"I'll tell you what I am going to do, Major Adams." The general spoke loudly, his words clear to all the junior officers and enlisted women on review. "I'm going to send a white first lieutenant down here to show you how to run this unit."

In a fraction of a second, Charity knew that if she didn't stand up to the general, she would lose the respect of her troops.

"Over my dead body," she answered. "Sir."

The general sputtered. "You'll hear from me, Adams." He dismissed her from his presence and walked to his limousine.

As Charity watched the vehicle drive away, it dawned on her. "I was in trouble."

The trouble arrived shortly. The general filed court-martial charges against her for insubordination.

Did she have any defense? For three days, Charity and her staff huddled in a "war conference" to find a strategy. She chose a bold move and drew up court-martial charges against the general.

Because he had threatened to replace her with a *white* officer, she accused him of using racist language. A memo from the army's highest command had cautioned officers against using language that called attention to racial segregation. The army didn't want to risk the enemy seeing disharmony among American troops. But the general had made a clear distinction between black and white officers.

It was "stretching a memorandum into a directive," Charity admitted privately, "but I had nothing to lose and everything to gain."

Her strategy worked. The general dropped his charges, saying a court-martial would require too many army resources.

It may have been a cop-out by the general, but Charity's gamble paid off. "I was not a fool; I did not pursue my charges against the general," she said. They still had to work together, and Charity was nervous the next time he came to visit the

6888th. But the general acted as if they'd never met before and seemed only concerned that the black women keep up their good work. "He was very pleasant," Charity said, "and you can be assured that I was."

It came as a surprise later when the general showed up to say goodbye before he rotated back to the States. "Adams, it's not easy for me to say what I've come to say." His voice was terse as he told her, "Working with you has been quite an education for me, especially about Negroes . . . It's been a long time since anyone challenged me, black or white, but you took me on. You outsmarted me, and I am proud that I know you."

Not long after Charity's run-in with the general, the 6888th dealt with another blow, a tragedy they shared with all Americans, the death of President Roosevelt, April 12, 1945.

The news was revealed to the WAC battalion as the women stood in formation that morning. "We continued to stand there stunned," Lucia Pitts said. "I remember finally stamping my foot and saying out loud, Oh, no!" She recalled that some women broke into tears.

A memorial was announced for the next day and they were dismissed. "We wandered blindly away," Lucia said. President Roosevelt had been respected for his government intervention programs that improved the economy and his employment of black officials. Now some women worried about what turn the war might take, and if and when they would go home. ★

CHAPTER 13

Mission Accomplished

Europe, 1945

By the end of April, the black women had nearly wiped out the backlog of mail in Birmingham, and they received news they would be redeployed to France to continue military mail distribution. "Morale was very high because everybody was looking forward to seeing as much of Europe as they could," Corporal Johnnie Walton said. Hopeful the war would end soon, the women looked forward to visiting historical sites and acting like tourists.

Members of the 6888th Central Postal Directory Battalion sorting and redirecting mail in Birmingham, England, 1945

The day finally came when the last letter in Birmingham was sent on its way. The 6888th Central Postal Directory Battalion had accomplished its mission and took only half the time expected! The African American women broke all records for redirecting U.S. military mail. Charity Adams felt fortunate to be their commanding officer, saying there were many women in the corps who would have been capable of the job. "My feeling of personal achievement was only a minute part of my pride in the unit."

"I was very proud of the Six Triple Eight," she said. "The women of the 6888th had ventured into a service area where

they were not really wanted; they assumed jobs that had normally been assigned to men; they [performed] in a valiant and praiseworthy manner; they had survived racial prejudice and discrimination with dignity. They were proud, and they had every right to be."

Charity left England to prepare for the battalion's move to France. After crossing the English Channel by boat, she caught a train for Paris the morning of May 8. Enjoying the French countryside, where patches of new green crops sprouted amid the scarred landscape of war, Charity began to note crowds gathering to cheer as the train swept through towns and villages. Not until she stepped off the train on the outskirts of Paris, where lively crowds jammed the streets, did she discover why everyone was celebrating.

Germany had surrendered. The Allies had won victory in Europe.

"From the moment we stepped off the train, everyone in the U.S. military uniform was subjected to the victory hysteria of the French. We were kissed on the cheek, sometimes on the lips, offered drinks, asked for souvenirs and if you had none, something was taken: your cap, insignia, epaulettes, even the braid on the sleeves." Charity had one of her shoelaces taken right off her foot.

Though the fighting was over, American military operations continued in Europe, and the 6888th deployed to Rouen, France. Crossing the choppy waters of the English

Members of the 6888th Central Postal Directory Battalion take part in a parade ceremony in honor of Joan of Arc at the marketplace where she was burned at the stake. May 27, 1945.

Channel on June 9, 1945, the women landed in Le Havre, a city turned to rubble by the German occupation and Allied bombing. Next they boarded a train for Rouen and their new quarters, Caserne Tallandier, an old French barracks that had most recently housed Nazis. Women whispered the chilling rumor that a German sniper had been buried in the center of the courtyard.

Their quarters featured familiar military double bunks, these constructed of army cots fitted into wood frames. "For mattresses, we were handed covers as we entered, which we had to stuff with fresh straw from a pile outside," Lucia Pitts said. "We found that when one lay down on it, it had a tendency to knot up, sticking one in the wrong places

Lieutenant Freda Le Beau of New Orleans, a PX officer, serves soda to Major Charity Adams of Columbia, South Carolina, at the grand opening of the WAC battalion's new snack bar.

and sometimes biting. We had no sheets, no pillows, just blankets ... but little stumps a WAC. Those who felt they had to have pillows made them out of extra blankets or coats or robes. Those who couldn't bear the rough blanket scratching their necks . . . found a piece of rag and folded it over the blanket edges."

Though they were roughing it, the close quarters in Rouen, as in Birmingham, fostered bonding among members of the battalion, and they developed a strong sense of sisterhood. "We worked; we accepted the bad along with the good," Margaret Jackson said. "There were a few complaints, but we knew what the circumstances were, that they were not permanent."

"We found the same conditions in France that we had found in England; the mail had been held up for months," Myrtle Rhoden said. "There was mail that was two or three years old. So we had to rewrap packages and reroute mail. The 6888th knitted together into one group, and we were determined to get the job done in France as we had in England."

The black women continued to be a novelty as they had been in England, and in France they were in much closer proximity to units of black male army troops. A few days after they arrived, a noncommissioned officer reported to

WACs sort packages taken from the mail sacks by French civilian employees at the 17th Base Post Office. Paris, France, November 7, 1945.

Major Charity Adams, "There are seven hundred twenty-five enlisted men for each enlisted woman and thirty-one male officers for each female officer."

"You mean in Europe?" Charity asked.

"No, ma'am, I mean outside our gates."

In the few days since the 6888th had arrived in France, "Word of our arrival had spread with the speed of sound," Charity said. "There were uniformed Negro soldiers as far as the eye could see when I looked out of the gate . . . Many had been away from home for several years, and just the sight of an American woman, regardless of race, was important, a connection with 'back home.'"

The women were happy to reconnect with men from home, friends, relatives, and sweethearts. Several couples had become engaged before leaving home and, now the war in Europe was over, they got married. But eventually, Charity had to limit the hours and numbers of male visitors, and women were assigned to help with security at the gates of Caserne Tallandier, so that the women could have privacy for such things as hanging their laundry out to dry.

In turn the women were curious about Europe, and now that the fighting had stopped, they could sightsee on their days off. The women participating in sports particularly enjoyed the move to the Continent. They traveled for competition, including a Ping-Pong tournament in Wiesbaden, Germany, and a softball tournament in Namur, Belgium. The

Private Ruth L. James of the battalion area is on duty at Caserne Tallandier gate, May 26, 1945. When the 6888th arrived in Rouen, France, in the spring of 1945, it caused a sensation among African American soldiers, who were so happy to see women from home that they crowded the gates daily, causing such a disruption that the battalion sometimes had to call in military police.

The 6888th had its own MPs, but they were not allowed to carry firearms. Instead, the women learned judo.

6888th softball team won the 1945 WAC Championship Softball Tournament in northern France.

After being barred from the all-star basketball tryouts in England, Gertrude Cruse Lavigne was eager to compete in the ETO Championship Basketball Tournament in Stuttgart, Germany. The 6888th team gathered at the train station with a number of other teams traveling to the tournament.

African American women, members of the Thirty-Second and Thirty-Third Companies' Women's Army Auxiliary Corps basketball team, playing a game of basketball at Fort Huachuca

African American WAC basketball players holding their trophy won at the ETO Championship Basketball Tournament in Rouen, France, 1945

"As we were ready to board the train, we were stopped and told that we would not be permitted to board." Gertrude refused to let discrimination end their chances. She made straight away to the office of General Lee, the commanding general of the Communications Zone, whom she hoped would have some influence, since the Allied forces were in charge of the trains.

"Upon stressing the urgency of our mission, we were permitted to see the general. I told him the situation about not being permitted to board the train for the tournament. He asked: 'Do you think you have a good team and can win?' Our reply was enthusiastically, 'Yes sir!' The general ordered a delay on the departure of that train and had his special car attached, and the 6888th team rode to Stuttgart in style all the way."

Gertrude and her teammates not only played in the tournament, they won the 1945 ETO Championship Basketball Tournament.

In October the 6888th moved again to be nearer the troops, this time to Paris. The women enjoyed the celebratory air of the French and the relief of the soldiers, done fighting for now, though the war continued in the Pacific. They also enjoyed much more lavish living quarters than their former barracks. The battalion was housed in two hotels where they had maid service and hotel meals. Their thick-carpeted rooms had large beds, walk-in closets and easy chairs. French families

befriended some members and invited them to their homes for dinner.

One family in France was so friendly to Ruth Jefferson Wright that later she named her son their surname, Lamont. And Bernice Thomas continued to keep in touch with friends she made in France after her return to the States. "I was treated fine; I stayed overnight with some of the French people. One woman in particular couldn't speak English, and I couldn't speak French, but we managed to get along. I would go to her home and we would have dinner."

By fall, a number of black women had reached the end of their tours of duty in the WAC and shipped back to the States to be discharged from the service. The unit shrank, and in December 1945 it was time for Charity to return stateside as well.

African American weekly newspaper *Call and Post* article on Lieutenant Colonel Charity Adams's retirement from the WAC. Happy at the lack of fanfare, "She simply moved into Cleveland, unattended and unannounced and went to work." September 21, 1946.

Her next posting, WAC headquarters at the Pentagon, didn't sound very exciting. She decided it was time to go home and get on with her life.

Arriving in New York harbor, Charity joined passengers rushing to get a glimpse of the Statue of Liberty. "The Lady" meant different things to different people: victory, liberty, reuniting with loved ones; for black WACs it also signaled a return to discrimination and bigotry. Charity focused on the positive, "For a few minutes most of us were joined . . . without discord, in order to see a statue that meant we were home . . . there was the satisfaction that I was one Negro WAC who had made it."

America gave its white soldiers a hero's welcome home. Black soldiers were mostly ignored. "[They] gave us our discharge papers and sent us home," Mary Crawford Ragland said. "There were no parades, no welcomes, no nothing."

Women like Charity Adams knew their worth. Practical and goal-oriented, they looked for jobs where their experience and talent would continue to make a difference. ★

Women!
Answer
America's
Call

SERVE IN THE W.A.A.C.

Charity Adams, the first African American officer in the Women's Army Auxiliary Corps, standing in uniform and pointing to a recruitment poster, 1943

CHAPTER 14

Black WACs Carry On

African American women joined the WACs to serve their country and to better their circumstances in life. Individual women gained mixed benefits from their time in the service during World War II. A number quit in dissatisfaction, like the black WACs who protested menial duties at Camp Breckinridge. Others like Gladys Thomas Anderson were disappointed they did not gain education or training in the army. "I went in as a stenographer clerk," she said, "and came out as a stenographer clerk."

A WAC laboratory technician conducts an experiment in the serology laboratory. Fort Jackson Station Hospital, Fort Jackson, South Carolina, 1944.

Corporal Ruth Hammond found the WAC did not improve her job prospects and standard of living as she had hoped. Nevertheless, she did not regret her military service. "I wanted to travel and I did. I met some very nice people; I saw some wonderful things."

WAC officer Martha Settle Putney researched the World War II experience of African American women in the army, writing several books and papers on the topic. She believed, as a whole, black women's service was an important step toward greater opportunity for blacks nationwide and helped lead to the making of the black middle class in America.

Another study of blacks in the World War II Women's Army Corps focused on women who served in the 6888th Central Postal Directory Battalion. Most of the women who participated in this 1996 study by historian Brenda L. Moore believed serving in the WAC had been a good experience for them and had helped smooth the way for their sisters who followed.

A number of black WACs gained material advantages in that their military service ranked them higher in the civil service points system, allowing them to qualify for higher-paying jobs in government after the war. Others were able to buy homes with the help of lower interest rates on loans offered through the Servicemen's Readjustment Act of 1944, known as the GI Bill. First Lieutenant Blanche Scott's wartime enlistment put her on a career track with secure financial footing, and she decided to stay in the army until she retired with the rank of major in 1965.

Military service improved many women's self-confidence and maturity. "I was young and had never worked or been away from home or experienced any of the real life outside of home," First Lieutenant Mildred Dupee Leonard said. "I had an opportunity to have four more years of maturity, with responsibilities. So when I came out of the military I really felt prepared [for adult life]."

"If it taught more discipline, I needed it," Private First Class Willie Whiting said. "I had resigned myself to the fact when

African American Private Hannah Wills developing an X-ray film in the X-ray laboratory at Post Hospital, Camp Breckinridge, 1943

I went in that there probably would be many times when something would be suggested that I would rather not do, but the military was not designed for me personally, so I did it."

WAC Allie Love Davis said being in the army made her "tough, disciplined, and self-controlled," and this benefited her personal and professional life after the war. Gladys Schuster Carter said, "I think the military gave me more direction. It gave me even more of a willingness to take on a job and to take on a challenge. I just think that I can do anything damn well if I put my mind to it. The military had a lot to do with that."

Private First Class Anna Tarryk said, "At first there were some disadvantages because when we [African American women] went in we were not totally respected. We had to fight the war on three fronts: first we had to fight segregation, second was the war, and third were the men," who were prejudiced against women. But she believed the military radically changed her perspective on life. "It gave me the opportunity to become independent and to mature quickly. It widened my horizons as far as people are concerned—learning about other cultures and stuff like that."

Corporal Odessa Marshall said she grew more independent and assertive during her time in the WAC, and those qualities led her to become an advocate for women's rights throughout her life.

Corporal Mary Daniels Williams was determined to raise her standard of life, and after discharge from the WAC she

went back to finish high school. "I knew that I was never gonna scrub another floor," Mary said. She went to college on the GI Bill, got a job as a clerk in welfare services, rose to secretary, then supervisor and eventually became a social worker.

Like Mary, many African American WACs gained higher education through the GI Bill. The law provided veterans low-interest loans to start a business, cash payments for tuition, and living expenses to attend university, high school, or vocational education, as well as one year of unemployment compensation. WACs Nealie and Leader Hoskins saved their army salaries and used the money to continue their education, both earning master's degrees. Dovey Johnson went to law school on the GI Bill, and went on to a distinguished law career focused on securing civil rights.

Black WAC officers gained leadership and organizational skills that empowered them to become civilian leaders. Before leaving the army, Charity Adams was promoted to Lieutenant Colonel, the highest rank possible in the WAC. Charity Adams had left graduate school to enter the WAC, and after the war she went back to school and finished her master's degree in vocational psychology, later becoming a dean at Tennessee Agricultural and Industrial State College and then Georgia State College. She also married and had children, and worked with agencies that enfranchised blacks and strengthened their communities. These included United Way, the Black

Leadership Development Program, the United Negro College Fund, the Urban League, the YWCA, and even the American Red Cross, an agency that had blatantly discriminated against her and her troops during World War II.

Charity Adams developed a strong sense of responsibility and personal dignity through her service in the WAC. "The future of women in the military seems assured," she wrote in 1989. "The barriers of sex and race were . . . still are, very difficult to overcome."

Finally, Recognition

Black WACs were among the bravest and most adventurous women in 1940s America. They interrupted careers, left family, friends, and loved ones, venturing into unknown and sometimes dangerous territory. They survived racial prejudice and discrimination with dignity.

Captain Dovey Johnson never forgot the day in 1945 when she joined the throng lining the sidewalks on Broadway to watch a grand parade in New York City. Japan had surrendered. The war was over. And the city turned out to welcome home U.S. Army General Jonathan Wainwright, who had survived four years in a Japanese prison camp.

"I've known moments of pure happiness in the course of my life, but never the sort of ecstasy that shot through me for three hours on the thirteenth of September, 1945. All around me, grown men wept openly and complete strangers hugged

The sidewalks of lower Broadway are jammed as the Wainwright motorcade goes north toward city hall, New York City, September 13, 1945.

U.S. President Barack Obama greets Alyce Dixon, the oldest living African American World War II veteran, in the Oval Office of the White House, Washington, D.C., October 27, 2014. Army Corporal Dixon died January 27, 2016, at the age of one hundred and eight.

each other. I stood a-tiptoe in my starched dress uniform, cheering and waving a flag . . . I kept saluting all afternoon, it seemed, as up and down Broadway the soldiers and sailors I passed along the long walk back to our car saluted me. Black and white alike, it made no difference that day."

Nearly sixty-five years after the war, in 2009, the U.S. Army officially recognized the contributions of the 6888th Central Postal Directory Battalion. Only a handful of the former soldiers remained alive. Three members of the 6888th attended the ceremony, Mary Crawford Ragland, Alyce Dixon, and Gladys Schuster Carter, each receiving a letter and certificate of commendation, showing appreciation for their outstanding service.

At the ceremony, Gladys spoke to black women in the current military, saying, "You are standing on our shoulders, but let me tell you what our pride is: seeing you young women who have succeeded since us."

The African American members of the Women's Army Corps proved that both blacks and women could make crucial contributions to the American military war effort and help assure victory. They survived racism and discrimination to make things easier for the black women who followed them. They earned the right to be remembered among those who have come to be called America's greatest generation. ★

Mary Ragland (*left*) and Alyce Dixon, both company clerks in the 6888th Central Postal Directory Battalion during World War II, pose for a photo with First Lady Michelle Obama during an event honoring Women's History Month and military families at Arlington National Cemetery's Women in Military Service for America Memorial, Arlington, Virginia, March 3, 2009. The ceremony also honored Esther Corcoran (*far right*), one of the first women to achieve the rank of Army lieutenant colonel.

Author's Note

Black WACs hoped their loyalty, courage, and excellent performance during war would gain them equal citizenship in peacetime. They believed their sacrifice and service would create opportunities for themselves and the African American women who followed. In many ways this has been true, but in the years following World War II, African Americans remained second-class citizens. Segregation continued to be the law throughout the southern states and the practice throughout the country.

New women's roles in the workplace credited to Rosie the Riveter and others during wartime applied mostly to white women. A large percentage of black women had worked outside the home before World War II, but the higher-paying postwar jobs available to women mo st often went to whites, even when qualified blacks applied. Many companies strictly refused to hire people of color, and even if African Americans were granted interviews and hired, they were barred from most management positions. According to historian Jacqueline Jones, the bitter fruit of African American women's efforts in World War II became fuel for the civil rights battles of the late 1950s and '60s. "[African American women] did begin to test the limits of their own collective strength in ways that would reverberate into the future."

Due to the sustained struggle for equal rights in the United States for both women and people of color, today black women in the American military are assigned the same jobs as whites and have the equal right with men to engage in combat. African American women are well represented in the U.S. Armed Forces, and a handful have been promoted to the upper ranks.

After World War II, a number of black women stayed in the WAC, and at the outbreak of the Korean War in 1950, they served in Okinawa, Japan, and the Philippines. In 1948 by executive order, President Harry S. Truman desegregated the armed forces, and the last segregated units were disbanded in 1954. An increasing number of African American women, mostly nurses, served in the Vietnam War (1964–1975). U.S. Army Nurse Corps Major Marie Rogers was awarded the Bronze Star by President Lyndon Johnson for distinguished service, and Diane Lindsay of the 95th Evacuation Hospital

became the first black nurse to receive the Soldier's Medal for heroism. In Operation Desert Storm (1990–1991), some 40 percent of the thirty-five thousand active duty women troops were African Americans. In the most recent conflicts involving the United States, the war in Afghanistan (2001–2014) and the war in Iraq (2003–2011), black female soldiers fought in the bloody streets of Baghdad and Kabul, comprising nearly one-third of all women in the U.S. Armed Forces.

As in Charity Adams's time, promotions continued to come slowly. But in 2016, the first African American woman was promoted to three-star general. Lieutenant General Nadja Y. West became the first African American to serve as army surgeon general, making her the army's first black woman to hold the rank of three-star general and the highest-ranking female graduate from West Point of any race.

In the twenty-first century, the military is possibly the most integrated institution in America, offering black women more breaks than they can find anywhere. It offers a steady job with good health care, childcare, and education.

Staff Sergeant Nikkia Y. Russell of Jersey City, New Jersey, enlisted in the army in 1999. Orphaned at age twelve, she was mad at the world, drinking, fighting, and skipping school. Then a program for troubled teens at Fort Dix, New Jersey, turned her around.

"See, everyone joins the army for different reasons," Nikkia said. "Some join to go to school, some because they come from a generation of soldiers and that tradition is important to them, and they are true patriots who love this country. Back then I was none of those things. I was simply just this young woman looking for a way out."

Joining the army was the best thing that ever happened to her, Nikkia said. "It taught me what TRUE self-respect meant; it taught me honor, discipline, and how to overcome obstacles, but most importantly it gave me the confidence I needed to be successful." She served ten years in the army, retiring in 2009.

Captain Trina L. Mitchell joined the Army Reserve Officers' Training Corps to pay for college in 1992. After graduation, during her two-year service in the medical corps, she realized many more benefits. "It was no longer about the

money but the relationships that had been forged. I began to love everything about the military. I didn't have to think about what to wear; I had a purpose in life, missions to complete."

The black WACs of the World War II era completed their mission. *Standing Up Against Hate: How Black Women in the Army Helped Change the Course of WWII* is my effort to help establish their memory solidly among the patriots and heroes of what has been called America's greatest generation.   ★

Glossary

army ranks—Enlisted Women: Private, Private Second Class, Private First Class; Corporal Officers: First Lieutenant, Second Lieutenant, Captain, Major, Lieutenant Colonel, Colonel, General

battalion—In relation to the U.S. Army, a ground force unit composed of a headquarters and four to six companies. Companies include sixty to two hundred soldiers.

Battle of the Bulge—The last major German offensive in World War II launched December 16, 1944 in the dense Ardennes forest region of Belgium, France, and Luxembourg. The attack caught the Allied forces off guard, and the Germans pushed into Allied territory, causing a huge bulge in the battle line across the western front in Europe. American forces suffered the highest casualties of any battle during the war before stopping the German advance on January 25, 1945.

court-martial—A judicial court for trying members of the armed services accused of offenses against military law.

entourage—A group of attendants or associates of a person of rank or importance.

GI—General infantry, name for army soldiers who engage in military combat on foot, majority of soldiers in World War II.

GI Bill—The Servicemen's Readjustment Act of 1944, commonly known as the GI Bill, provided a range of benefits for returning World War II veterans including cash payments for tuition and living expenses to attend university, high school, or vocational education, low-cost mortgages, low-interest loans to start a business, and one year of unemployment pay.

insubordination—Disobeying the command of a military officer of higher rank than oneself.

Jim Crow—Formal system of state and local laws enforcing racial segregation in the American South 1877–1965.

Ku Klux Klan (KKK)—A white supremacist organization (1866–present day) known for acts of terrorism—including murder, lynching, arson, rape, and bombing—to oppose the granting of civil rights to African Americans.

MP—Military police, the law enforcement arm of the U.S. Army.

mutiny—Rebellion against the proper authorities, especially by soldiers or sailors against their officers.

National Association for the Advancement of Colored People (NAACP)—African American organization formed in 1909 to ensure the political, educational, social, and economic equality as rights of all persons and to eliminate race-based discrimination.

National Council of Negro Women—A nonprofit organization founded by Mary McLeod Bethune in 1935 with the mission to advance the opportunities and the quality of life for African American women, their families, and communities.

Nazi—The twentieth-century German Nazi Party, the Nazi state headed by Adolf Hitler, or a member thereof.

post-traumatic stress disorder—The mental illness characterized by flashbacks, depression, anxiety, nightmares, and avoidance behavior in reaction to surviving a terrifying event, such as combat.

rank—A system of hierarchical relationships in the armed forces; designations of leaderships and responsibility for personnel, equipment, and mission grows with each increase in rank.

segregation—The enforced separation of different racial groups in a country, community, or establishment.

spit and polish—Thorough or exaggerated cleaning and polishing, especially by a soldier.

ward—A division in a hospital; a large room in a hospital for the care of patients often requiring similar treatment.

Women's Army Corps (WAC)—Women's branch of the U.S. Army. The WAC was disbanded in 1978, and all units were integrated with male units.

Women's Auxiliary Army Corps (WAAC)—Women's branch of the U.S. Army created by Congress May 14, 1942. Auxiliary to the army, WAACs deployed without the same benefits as soldiers. If injured, they might not receive the same care. If captured, they could not expect the same rights and protections. The WAAC was converted to full army status as the Women's Army Corps in July 1943.

Time Line

December 7, 1941: Japan bombs Pearl Harbor, inciting the United States to join World War II.

May 14, 1942: Congress approves bill creating the Women's Auxiliary Army Corp (WAAC).

July 19, 1942: Charity Adams arrives at Fort Des Moines, Iowa, to begin WAAC officer candidate training.

August 7, 1942–February 9, 1943: Battle of Guadalcanal, the first major offensive and decisive victory for the Allies in the Pacific theater of World War II.

August 29, 1942: First class of WAAC officers commissioned, including thirty-nine African Americans.

December 1942: First WAACs assigned duty at army posts around the country, including a detachment of African Americans sent to Fort Huachuca, Arizona.

June 25, 1943: Twenty-one African American WAACs strike against unfair duty assignments at Camp Breckinridge, Kentucky. Six women refuse orders to return to duty and resign from the WAAC.

July 3, 1943: New law converts WAAC to the Women's Army Corp (WAC), making it part of the army, rather than an auxiliary corps serving the army.

July 1943: First battalion of white WACs to serve overseas arrive in London, England.

June 6, 1944: D-day, a major turning point in the war in Europe when Allies invade German-occupied France in the largest amphibious attack in history.

December 16, 1944–January 25, 1945: The Battle of the Bulge, Germany's last major offensive in World War II.

January 25, 1945: Major Charity Adams ordered to overseas duty in England.

February 11, 1945: First contingent of black WACs, the 6888th Central Postal Directory Battalion, arrives for overseas duty in Great Britain.

March 1945: Fifty-four black WACs strike claiming unfair duty assignments at Fort Devens, Massachusetts. Four women are court-martialed after refusing to work.

May 7, 1945: Germany surrenders. The war in Europe is over.

May 1945: The 6888th Postal Battalion moves to Rouen, France.

August 15, 1945: Japan surrenders. World War II ends.

October 1945: The 6888th reassigned to Paris, France.

December 1945: Major Adams returns to the United States.

December 26, 1945: Charity Adams promoted to lieutenant colonel, the highest rank attainable in the WAC.

Notes

Chapter 1: Reporting for War Duty

2   "Due to the hardships . . . unhappy-looking lot" Charity Adams Earley, *One Woman's Army: A Black Officer Remembers the WAC* (College Station, TX: Texas A & M University Press, 1989) 141.

3   "Don't let being an officer . . . slaves to my people" Ibid., 108.

3   "It was frightening . . . gotten ourselves into" Avis Thomas-Lester, "Neither Rain, Nor Racial Bias," *Washington Post*, February 26, 2009, www.washingtonpost.com/wp-dyn/content/article /2009/02/25/AR2009022503571.html.

4   "We were both appalled . . . and intimidated" Margaret Y. Jackson letter to Martha S. Putney, 1.

5   "There were packages . . . cats in there" Janet Sims-Woods, "We Served America, Too! Black Women in the Women's Army Corps during World WAR II," *Journal of the Afro-American Historical Society*, vol. 13, nos. 3 and 4, 1994, 171.

5   "Letters were a great comfort . . . the war without it" www.pbs .org/thewar/detail_5185.htm.

Chapter 2: Second-Class Citizens

12   "If you lived during . . . do their part" Brenda L. Moore, *To Serve My Country, To Serve My Race: The Story of the Only African American WACs Stationed Overseas During World War II* (New York: New York University Press, 1996) 34.

13   "This war is not . . . in the homes" Cong. Rec. (March 17, 1942) 2592–2593, abmceducation.org/sites/default/files/activity /Congressional-Record-Excerpts.pdf.

17   "Even with the knowledge . . . I had to offer" Earley, *One Woman's Army*, 15.

18   "That is when the fear . . . I would have backed out" Ibid., 16.

19   "Race, color, age . . . pushed aside" Ibid., 19.

20   "I, a Negro . . . most unusual situation" Ibid., 16.

20 "Will all the colored girls move over to this side" Ibid., 19.

20 "It did not occur . . . be called by name" Ibid., 20.

Chapter 3: Becoming Officers Together

24 "I've never eaten . . . going to start now" Carol Rust, "We Served America, Too: Blacks in the WAC Were Up Against More Than Nazis," *Houston Chronicle*, June 6, 1994, 1.

24 "With those signs . . . something's wrong" Dovey Roundtree, "My Childhood," YouTube interview, National Visionary Leadership Project, June 10, 2009, youtu.be/lUFnieBLgkE.

24 "Everyone felt depressed . . . There was definitely two" Ibid.

25 "We cried, we didn't sleep . . . I didn't say it as a joke" Ibid.

25 "Very definitely . . . hurt to the core" Ibid.

25 "Mrs. Hobby [who was white] told the . . . same kind of treatment" Rust, "We Served America, Too," 1.

25 "We are making history . . . a challenging responsibility" Cheryl Mullenbach, *Double Victory: How African American Women Broke Race and Gender Barriers to Help Win World War II* (Chicago: Chicago Review Press, 2013) 95–96.

26 "She . . . told us that . . . a beautiful job" Moore, *To Serve My Country*, 54.

26 "From now on you . . . that it stands for" Katie McCabe and Dovey Johnson Roundtree, *Justice Older Than the Law: The Life of Dovey Johnson Roundtree*, Margaret Walker Alexander Series in African American Studies (Jackson, MS: University Press of Mississippi, 2009) 58.

27 "A funny thing happened . . . girl from Georgia" Rust, "We Served America, Too," 1.

27 "You got down to . . . only my backside" Martha Putney, "Experiencing War: Stories from the Veterans History Project," Library of Congress, March 26, 2004, http://memory.loc.gov /diglib/vhp-stories/loc.natlib.afc2001001.12523/transcript? ID=mv0001.

30 "I discovered in those . . . we celebrated together" McCabe and Roundtree, *Justice*, 59.

30 "But what they didn't . . . studying those manuals" Roundtree, "My Childhood."

32 "We saluted like mad . . . idea what to do" Earley, *One Woman's Army*, 40.

32 "I did not like physical training . . . without falling down" Earley, *One Woman's Army*, 33. (caption)

33 "I took to drill the way a duck takes to water" and entire incident relating to drill, Ibid., 33–34.

33 "with heads high . . . breathing defiance to Hitler, Hirohito, and Mussolini" Mullenbach, *Double Victory*, 98.

34 Earley, *One Woman's Army*, 38.

35 "Whatever doubts we . . . fraternity of officers" Earley, *One Woman's Army*, 43.

Chapter 4: Black Women Persist

38 "That, I determined . . . in the Deep South" McCabe and Roundtree, *Justice*, 62.

38 "Was that opportunity precisely . . . compared to that?" Ibid., 59.

38 "they told me . . . anything about it" Janet Sims-Wood, "Service Life in the Women's Army Corps and Afro-American WACs" in Paula Nassen Poulos, ed., *A Woman's War Too: U.S. Women in the Military in World War II* (Washington, D.C.: National Archives and Records Administration, 1996) 130.

39 "I'm sitting there with the very bill still with the ink kind of moist on it" Ibid.

39 "wild goose chase . . . the very thing the Allies are fighting against" Mary Elnora White to War Department, July 1, 1943, Box 50, Series 54, RG 165, NA.

40 "Here I am, for instance" White, Mary Elnora, Letter to United States War Department. Washington, D.C., July 1, 1943.

41 "because it called for general information" Hampf, Michaela,

M.. *Release a Man for Combat: The Women's Army Corps During World War II*. Böhlau Verlag (Germany), 2010, p. 206.

41   "in public places giving public speeches" Mattie E. Treadwell, *United States Army in World War II: Special Studies: The Women's Army Corps* (Washington, D.C.: U.S. Government Printing Office, 1954), 594.

41–42   "I felt like he . . . for my country, too" Rust, "We Served America, Too," 1.

42   "I felt that . . . particularly for black women" Moore, *To Serve My Country*, 10.

42   "I was going nowhere fast . . . a totally new life" Moore, *To Serve My Country*, 12.

43   "I wanted to go to motor corps to drive a truck" Ernestine Woods, letter to Martha S. Putney, NABWH_038 Series 3 Box 2 Folder 7.

43   "Again, I waited anxiously and breathlessly" Ibid.

46   "happy not to be . . . our bunks and cried" Ibid.

46–47   "a lot of girls . . . cooks' and bakers' school" Moore, *To Serve My Country*, 66.

46   "I would appreciate . . . reception rooms with n—" George Mahon letter to Colonel Howard Clark, II, Chief of Operations Service, Headquarters, WAAC, April 22, 1943.

47   "temporary and practically unavoidable" Leisa D. Meyer, *Creating GI Jane: Sexuality and Power in the Women's Army Corps During World War II* (New York: Columbia University Press, 1997) 68.

47   "I knew there was . . . all succeeded together" Earley, *One Woman's Army*, 60.

49   "in the place of the man behind the gun" McCabe and Roundtree, *Justice*, 59.

49   "There are, I am persuaded . . . regulations on the base" Ibid., 59.

Chapter 5. Every Victory Counts

52   "soldier with the best men" Mullenbach, *Double Victory*, 105.

55   "These young women . . . able-bodied men" Martha S. Putney,

When the Nation Was in Need: Blacks in the Women's Army Corps During World War II (Metuchen, NJ: The Scarecrow Press, Inc, 1992) 77.

56   "The spirit of the WACs . . . the base command" Ibid., 83.

58   "We decided that . . . what we called them" "Experiencing War: Stories from the Veterans History Project."

58   "purified . . . If I'd ever had . . . might have resigned" McCabe and Roundtree, *Justice*, 59.

58–59   "When can we swim?" and following quotes about desegregating the Fort Des Moines swimming pool: "Experiencing War: Stories from the Veterans History Project."

60   "I don't think anybody . . . women in uniform before" Jill M. Sullivan, *Bands of Sisters: U.S. Women's Military Bands During World War II* (Lanham, MD: Scarecrow Press, 2011) 29.

61   "They made us feel . . . if we were famous" Martha S. Putney, "The Women's Army Corps Black Band: A Historical Note" (Washington, D.C.: Conference of Army Historians, 1992) 11.

61   "On Saturday nights . . . was jazzier than theirs" Sullivan, *Bands of Sisters*, 34.

64   "To disband now . . . of the Negro WACs" Ibid., 36.

65   "lights go out on the post on a star-studded night" Putney, "The Women's Army Corps Black Band," 11.

Chapter 6: Black Soldiers Get the Dirty Work

68   "insubordination . . . [offense] in the service": Testimony of Colonel Clyde Parmelee, Report of Proceedings of Board of Officers, 3562nd Service Unit, Section 2, WAAC Camp Breckinridge, Kentucky, June 26, 1943.

69   "In a pronounced southern accent . . . Congress that commissioned you'" Oral interview, University of Nevada Oral History Archive: War Stories: Veterans Remember World War II, 82–83, contentdm.library.unr.edu/cdm/search/collection /unohp/searchterm/world%20war/field/unohp/mode/all/conn /and/order/oral.

70 "well-educated Negro women . . . sweeping warehouse floors" Putney, *When the Nation Was in Need*, 80.

70 "Most of these girls . . . in civilian life" Ibid.

71 "The crowded living . . . can help end hostilities" Earley, *One Woman's Army*, 79.

71 "I'm hoping you could . . . dark skinned woman" Violet A. McAtee letter to Eleanor Roosevelt, September 30, 1942.

72 "Gardiner General Hospital . . . as nurses' assistants" Putney, *When the Nation Was in Need*, 39.

72–74 "choice assignment" and "It was newly constructed . . . beautiful out there" and "Now you're going . . . tolerate you" and "In fact . . . done an efficient job" Martha Putney, "Experiencing War: Stories from the Veterans History Project," Library of Congress, March 26, 2004.

Chapter 7: Black WACs Strike for Fair Jobs

76 "black WACs taking temperatures" *United States* v. *Morrison*. Proceedings of a General Court-Martial, Fort Devens, M.A., March 19, 1945; 318.

76 "They are here to scrub . . . all the dirty work" United States v. Morrison, Anna C., Green, Mary E., Young, Alice E., Murphy, Johnnie, A. (Proceedings of a General Court-Martial, Fort Devens, Massachusetts, March 19, 1945) 201.

76 "The uniforms were even . . . complete white uniforms" Ibid., 202.

77 "[I] never saw any white . . . and been a maid" Ibid., 162.

77 "They want no blacks working at the motor pool" Ibid., 180.

78 "mutiny" United States Army Commanding Major General Sherman Miles' letter to the Judge Advocate General of the Army, War Department, Washington, D.C., March 28, 1945.

79 "Any person subject to . . . court-martial may direct" Revision of the Articles of War (Committee on Military Affairs, Senate Calendar No. 122, 64th Congress, 1st session, February 9,

1916) 8.

79   "I now give each . . . following direct order" United States v.
Morrison, charges and specifications, 2.

79   "I will take a court-martial" Ibid., 216.

79   "I was hysterical . . . lay down and die" Ibid., 116.

79   "If it will help . . . put my name down" Ibid., 119.

79   "I would take death before I would go back to work" Ibid., 241.

80   "They enlisted to see . . . promised to Americans" Ibid., 319–320.

81   "They do practically nothing . . . is altogether different"
Ibid., 207.

82   "why so many thousands . . . flourishing at home" Meyer,
Creating GI Jane, 99.

Chapter 8: Violence Targets Black WACs

83   "It's strange how you . . . was work and serve" Andrea Hunt
and Heidi Dehncke, "We Too Served: Black Women in WWII,"
unpublished paper (Washington, D.C.: Martha Settle Putney
Collection on the Women's Army Corps, National Archives for
Black Women's History, 1991) 7.

86   "Daddy got out . . . men light a cigarette" Earley, *One Woman's
Army*, 63.

86   "couldn't do anything about men parked on the street" Ibid., 63.

87   "of anger a 'n—' . . . people to salute her" Ibid., 103.

90   "kill'em, kill'em" Meyer, *Creating GI Jane*, 95.

90   "Git up and git out . . . for white people" Harry McAlpin, "Beat by
cops: WACs to stand trial, violated Ky. Jim Crow," *Indianapolis
Recorder*, August 8, 1945, 1

90–91   "When we tell n—s to move, we mean for them to git" Ibid., 1.

90   "they never moved" Constance Curtis, "N.Y. WAC Beaten by
Dixie Cop" *New Amsterdam-Star News*, July 28, 1945, unknown
page.

92   "I guess you wondered . . . are very real" Ibid., unknown page.

92   "stamp of approval on the acts of prejudiced Southerners" "Army

Should Act," *New York Age*, August 18, 1945, 6.

93   "Sir, you're not going . . . pawing in my mouth" Elsie Oliver's
      quotes about dentist, Moore, *To Serve My Country*, 74.

93   "Each time I went . . . of my being AWOL" Hunt and Dehncke,
      "We Too Served," 6.

94   "The WAAC was . . . to accept the challenge" Ibid.

Chapter 9: Called for Overseas Duty

97   "WAC units are shipped . . . requested to date" Harry McAlpin,
      "Turn Down Negro WACs for Overseas Service," *Chicago
      Defender*, February 5, 1944, 5.

97   "The truth was . . . any new venture" Earley, *One Woman's Army*,
      122.

98–99 "I think I would have climbed . . . where I was born" Moore, *To
      Serve My Country*, 18–19.

98   "Who would have ever . . . It was very exciting" Ibid., 19.

99   "She told me that . . . shipment at four p.m. today" Elsie Oliver
      anecdote, Ibid., 18.

100   "'Finally I went to . . . because of your race." Oral interview,
      University of Nevada Oral History Archive, 83.

100   "Salutes were slow . . . great reluctance" Earley, *One Woman's
      Army*, 134.

101   "Every conceivable kind . . . stared at us" Ibid., 135.

101   "It was safe . . . did we exhale" Ibid., 137–138.

102   "They say if you raise up . . . save your life" Moore, *To Serve My
      Country*, 100.

102   "I wanted to go . . . jail, so I stayed" Avis Thomas-Lester, "Neither
      Rain, Nor Racial Bias," www.washingtonpost.com/wp-dyn
      /content/story/2009/02/25/ST2009022503597.html.

102   "We had a mock ship . . . up and get them" Moore, *To Serve My
      Country*, 100.

102–103 "We were trained . . . of warfare training" Ibid., 100.

103   "The eyes of the world" Ibid., 99.

103   "We could either . . . and receive ridicule" Ibid., 99.

Chapter 10: The 6888th Goes to Europe

105 "It was loaded . . . needed for war" Moore, *To Serve My Country*, 105.

106 "All I remember is that I was sick the whole time" Ibid., 105.

107 "It lasted, they tell me . . . It just stopped" Ibid., 107.

108 "The strange thing about . . . lucky, I guess, lucky" Martha Putney, "Experiencing War," memory.loc.gov/diglib/vhp-stories /loc.natlib.afc2001001.04741/transcript?ID=sr0001.

108 "The farmlands looked . . . swept by a broom" Moore, *To Serve My Country*, 111.

108–109 "It was cold . . . helmet most of the time" Ibid., 113.

109 "I had never been . . . and poorly ventilated" Ibid., 112.

109 "With all the 'spit and polish' . . . " entire conversation between Major Adams and General Lee, Earley, *One Woman's Army*, 139.

110 "Ten minutes before . . . [we were] early" Ibid., 142.

111 "We were just stymied by the mail stacked all over" Moore, *To Serve My Country*, 114.

111–112 "Some Americans didn't understand . . . get them their mail" Avis Thomas-Lester. "Neither Rain, Nor Racial Bias,"

114 "There was part of the history of these men on the files . . . determined to try to find him" Elizabeth M. Collins, "Sorting the Mail, Blazing a Trail: African-American women in WWII," www.army.mil/article/181382/sorting_the_mail_blazing_a_ trail_african_american_women_in_wwii, accessed April 25, 2017.

114 "The wives and sweethearts . . . send back—deceased" Samantha L. Quigley, "A Life of Note: Alyce Dixon," *On Patrol*, Spring 2012, usoonpatrol.org/archives/2012/02/29/a-life-of-note-alyce-dixon.

115 "They could take a box . . . how good they were" Sims-Wood, "We Served America, Too!" 172.

115 "One week you had . . . but we managed" Moore, *To Serve My Country*, 181.

Chapter 11: Welcomed as Equals

118   "They have lively minds . . . proper reserve": Putney, *When the Nation Was in Need*, 105.

118   "At Fort Oglethorpe, we . . . like kings and queens" Meyer, *Creating GI Jane*, 95.

119   "There were always invitations and parties to attend" Putney, *When the Nation Was in Need*, 104.

119   "[The white soldiers] started . . . and were thrown out" Ibid., 121.

119   "This wonderful English family took me in . . . It was beautiful" Moore, *To Serve My Country*, 121–122.

119   "We realize that your . . . hotel all to themselves" Earley, *One Woman's Army*, 163.

122   "But more important . . . only after our arrival" Jackson letter to Martha S. Putney.

122   "We had some very . . . and pride and race" Moore, *To Serve My Country*, 121.

123   "She was liked. Everybody admired her for who she was" Ibid., 132.

123   "She had brains and beauty. She had it all." Ibid., 132.

123   "Even before leaving Fort Oglethorpe . . . could look their best" Earley, *One Woman's Army*, 145.

123–124   "just like back home" Ibid., 146.

124   "Members of our unit . . . recreational equipment we had" Ibid., 146.

125   "Anyone who wanted . . . not in Buckingham Palace" Moore, *To Serve My Country*, 128.

129   "That incident really brought . . . never heard from her again" Ibid., 181.

129   "We realized that we had self-worth, a right to be proud and dignified" Ibid.,194.

Chapter 12. A Challenge to Leadership

132–133   "Adams, where are the other personnel . . ." Major Charity Adams's conversation with general, Earley, *One Woman's Army*, 160.

133 "war conference" Ibid., 161.

133 "stretching a memorandum . . . everything to gain" Ibid., 161.

133 "I was not a fool; I did not pursue my charges against the general" Ibid., 161.

134 "He was very pleasant . . . assured that I was" Ibid., 162.

134 "Adams . . . It's not easy . . . proud that I know you" Ibid., 192.

134 "We continued to stand . . . wandered blindly away" Moore, *To Serve My Country*, 139.

Chapter 13: Mission Accomplished

135 "Morale was very high . . . Europe as they could" Earley, *One Woman's Army*, 141.

136–137 "My feeling of personal achievement . . . every right to be" Ibid., 183.

137 "From the moment we . . . braid on the sleeves" Ibid., 172.

138–139 "For mattresses . . . the blanket edges" Moore, *To Serve My Country*, 117.

139 "We worked; we accepted . . . were not permanent" Ibid., 141.

140 "We found the same conditions . . .we had in England" Ibid., 120.

141 "There are seven hundred twenty-five enlisted men . . . outside our gates . . . Word of our arrival had spread with the speed of sound . . . connection with 'back home'" Ibid., 175.

145 "As we were ready . . . style all the way." Gertrude Cruse Lavigne conversation with General Lee, Moore, *To Serve My Country*, 127.

146 "I was treated fine . . . would have dinner" Ibid., 124.

147 "For a few minutes . . . WAC who had made it" Earley, *One Woman's Army*, 208.

147 "[They] gave us our . . . no welcomes, no nothing" Avis Thomas-Lester, "Neither Rain, Nor Racial Bias," www.washingtonpost.com/wp-dyn/content/story/2009/02/25/ST2009022503597.html.

147   "She simply moved . . . went to work," "Race's First Women Lt. Colonel in Veterans' Administration Post," *Call and Post*, Cleveland, Ohio: September 21, 1946, 11A.

Chapter 14: Black WACs Carry On

149   "I went in as a stenographer clerk . . . and came out as a stenographer clerk" Moore, *To Serve My Country*, 155.

150   "I wanted to travel . . . some wonderful things" Ibid., 154.

151   "I was young . . . prepared [for adult life]" Ibid., 156.

151–154   "If it taught . . . personally, so I did it" Ibid., 156.

154   "tough, disciplined, and self-controlled" Ibid., 157.

154   "I think the military . . . lot to do with that" Ibid., 156–157.

154   "At first there were . . . and stuff like that" Ibid., 157.

155   "I knew that I was never gonna scrub another floor" Ibid., 171.

156   "The future of women . . . difficult to overcome" Earley, *One Woman's Army*, ix.

156–159   "I've known moments . . . no difference that day" McCabe and Roundtree, *Justice*, 74.

159   "You are standing . . . succeeded since us" Avis Thomas-Lester, "Neither Rain, Nor Racial Bias," www.washingtonpost.com /wp-dyn/content/story/2009/02/25/ST2009022503597.html.

163   "[African American women] did begin to . . . reverberate into the future" Maureen Honey, ed., *Bitter Fruit: African American Women in World War II* (Columbia, MO: University of Missouri Press, 1999) 31.

165–166   "See everyone joins . . . to be successful." Nikkia Y. Russell, email correspondence with the author June 22, 2017 to July 19, 2017.

166   "It was no longer . . . missions to complete." Trina L. Mitchell, email correspondence with the author June 21, 2017.

Select Bibliography

Books and Periodicals

*denotes books for young people
**denotes fiction

Earley, Charity Adams. *One Woman's Army: A Black Officer Remembers the WAC*. College Station, TX: Texas A & M University Press, 1989.

Hampf, Michaela, M.. *Release a Man for Combat: The Women's Army Corps During World War II*. Böhlau Verlag (Germany), 2010.

Holley, Lila. *Camouflaged Sisters: Revealing Struggles of the Black Woman's Military Experience*. Baltimore: Purposely Created, 2015.

Honey, Maureen, ed. *Bitter Fruit: African American Women in World War II*. Columbia, MO: University of Missouri Press, 1999.

Johnson, Jesse J., ed. *Black Women in the Armed Forces 1942–1974: A Pictorial History*. Chicago: Johnson, 1974.

McCabe, Katie and Dovey Johnson Roundtree. *Justice Older Than the Law: The Life of Dovey Johnson Roundtree*. Margaret Walker Alexander Series in African American Studies. Jackson, MS: University Press of Mississippi, 2009.

Meyer, Leisa D. *Creating GI Jane: Sexuality and Power in the Women's Army Corps During World War II*. New York: Columbia University Press, 1997.

Moore, Brenda L. *To Serve My Country, To Serve My Race: The Story of the Only African American WACs Stationed Overseas During World War II*. New York: New York University Press, 1996.

Morris, Robert V. *Black Faces of War: A Legacy of Honor from the American Revolution to Today*. Minneapolis: Zenith Press, 2011.

*Mullenbach, Cheryl. *Double Victory: How African American Women Broke Race and Gender Barriers to Help Win World War II*. Women of Action. Chicago: Chicago Review Press, 2013.

Phillips, Kimberley L. *WAR! What Is It Good For? Black Freedom Struggles and the U.S. Military from World War II to Iraq*. Chapel Hill, NC: The University of North Carolina Press, 2012.

Poulos, Paula Nassen, ed. *A Woman's War Too: U.S. Women in the Military in World War II*. Washington, D.C.: National Archives and Records Administration, 1996.

Putney, Martha S. *When the Nation Was in Need: Blacks in the Women's Army Corps During World War II*. Metuchen, NJ: Scarecrow Press, 1992.

Sims-Woods, Janet. "We Served America, Too! Black Women in the Women's Army Corps during World WAR II." *Journal of the Afro-American Historical Society*, vol. 13, nos. 3 and 4 (1994).

**Smith, Sherri, L. *Flygirl*. New York: Speak, 2010.

Sullivan, Jill M. *Bands of Sisters: U.S. Women's Military Bands during World War II*. Lanham, MD: Scarecrow Press, 2011.

Treadwell, Mattie E. *United States Army in World War II: Special Studies: The Women's Army Corps*. Washington, D.C.: U.S. Government Printing Office, 1954.

*Weatherford, Doris. *American Women and World War II. History of Women in America*. Oxford, UK: Fact on File, Inc., 1990.

Websites

Bellafaire, Judith A. *The Women's Army Corps: A Commemoration of World War II Service*, U.S. Army Center of Military History, www.history.army.mil /brochures/WAC/WAC.HTM.

Library of Congress Veterans History Project, Essie Dell O'Bryant Woods Collection, memory.loc.gov/diglib/vhp/bib/loc.natlib.afc2001001.04741.

Library of Congress Veterans History Project, "Experiencing War: Stories from the Veterans History Project," Library of Congress, March, 26, 2004, interview with Martha Putney, memory.loc.gov/diglib/vhp-stories /loc.natlib.afc2001001.12523/transcript?ID=mv0001.

National Archives and Records Administration, Pictures of African Americans during World War II, www.archives.gov/research/african-americans /ww2-pictures.

National Visionary Leadership Project, *Dovey Roundtree: The Women's Army Auxiliary Corps*, interview with black WAAC, youtu.be/P84q-1Xs5io.

The National Association of Black Military Women, www.nabmw.com /1095446.html.

Thomas-Lester, Avis, "Neither Rain Nor Racial Bias," The *Washington Post's* coverage of ceremony honoring the 6888th Central Postal Directory Battalion, February 26, 2009, www.washingtonpost.com/wp-dyn /content/article/2009/02/25/AR2009022503571.html.

United States Department of State, article members of the 6888th Central Postal Directory Battalion, March 5, 2009, iipdigital.usembassy.gov /st/english/article/2009/03/20090305131232gcirofo0.3113367 .html#axzz2KzAE8UBQ.

Image Credits

Pages iix: U.S. Army. **Pages xii, 14–15, 28–29, 31, 34, 40, 44–45, 48, 50, 52, 53, 54, 57, 84–85, 124, 128, 138, 139, 140, 142–143, 150:** National Archives and Records Administration. **Page 3:** United States Department of Defense. **Pages 4, 8, 36, 111:** Courtesy of the TWU Libraries Woman's Collection, Texas Woman's University, Denton, Texas. **Pages 6, 106–107:** United States Signal Corps. **Page 10:** Everett Collection Inc./Alamy Stock Photo. **Page 11:** Judith Earley. **Page 16:** Dwight D. Eisenhower Presidential Library. **Pages 18–19, 66, 78, 80–81, 91:** Courtesy of the Afro-American Newspapers Archives and Research Center. **Pages 22, 104, 144, 148, 152–153:** Schomburg Center for Research in Black Culture, New York Public Library, Photographs and Prints Division, Astor, Lenox and Tilden Foundations. **Page 24:** Katie McCabe. **Page 26:** Getty Images/Bettmann. **Pages 32, 157:** Library of Congress. **Page 56:** Martha (Settle) Putney Collection, Women's Memorial Foundation Collection. **Pages 59, 65:** National Parks Service, Mary McLeod Bethune Council House National History Site, National Archives for Black Women's History. **Pages 62–63, 88–89:** U.S. Army Women's Museum. **Pages 73, 77:** *Chicago Defender*. **Page 87:** *New Amsterdam News*, Copyright Clearance Center. **Page 96:** Alyce Dixon. **Pages 98, 120–121:** U.S. Army Center of Military History. **Page 98:** National Association of Black Military Women. **Page 101:** Imperial War Museum. **Page 103:** Mirrorpix Photo Archives. **Pages 112, 130:** Gladys (Thomas) Anderson Collection, Women's Memorial Foundation Collection. **Page 114:** U.S. Postal Museum. **Page 115:** CriticalPast. **Page 126–127:** Mildred (Sanders) Young Collection, Women's Memorial Foundation Collection. **Page 136:** Lawrence E. Walker Foundation Collection. **Page 146:** *Cleveland Call & Post*. **Page 158:** Official White House photo by Pete Souza. **Pages 160–161:** Official White House photo by Joyce N. Boghosian.

Acknowledgments

I'm so very grateful to my editor Howard Reeves for having a vison for this story and guiding me toward it. Additional gratitude to the team at Abrams Books for Young Readers for producing this beautiful book, including Emily Daluga, Masha Gunic, Amy Vreeland, Pamela Notarantonio, Erich Lazar, and the Marketing and Publicity team: Nicole Schaefer, Tessa Meischeid, Trish McNamara O'Neill, and Jenny Choy.

Special thank you to agent Stephen Fraser; to writer and podcaster (*Minorities in Publishing*) Jennifer N. Baker, for reading the manuscript and helping me see it with new eyes; to Stanley and Judith Earley, for sharing thoughts and memories of their mother Charity Adams Earley and for the photo of her as a child. Additionally, I'm so very grateful to Major General Marcia M. Anderson, Army (Ret.) for writing the foreword to *Standing Up Against Hate*.

This book would not have been possible without so many people helping me with research and photo procurement. I am so grateful to Mollie Coffey, Sumi Shadduck and Michelle Walker, Spokane Public Library; Holly Reed, National Archives and Records Administration, Still Picture Reference Team; Tavis Anderson, archivist, National Archives at St. Louis; Brenda L. Moore, University at Buffalo, SUNY; Kenneth J. Chandler, archivist, National Park Service, National Archives for Black Women's History; Ashley N. Robertson, curator/director, Mary McLeod Bethune Foundation, Megan B. Dwyre, Textual Reference, National Archives at College Park, Maryland; Kimberly L. Johnson and Shelia Bickle, Texas Woman's University Archives; Gary Dangerfield, chief external communications, Joint Base Lewis-McChord; Britta K. Granrud, curator of collections, Women in Military Service to America Memorial Foundation; Jonelyn Whales, National Association of Black Military Women; author Katie McCabe; Sheila Scott, *Afro-American*; Angela Ford, *Chicago Defender*; Kathy Struss, audiovisual archivist, Dwight D. Eisenhower Presidential Library and Museum; Andrea Felder and David Rosado, New York Public Library, permissions and reproduction services; historian NormHaskett, ww2days.com; Andy Erickson, CriticalPast.com;

Acknowledgments

Lawrence E. Walker, director and producer of the film *Sweet Georgia Brown*, www.purehistory.org.

To Major Jeanne Farrell, Army (Ret.) and Colonel Robert Farrell, Army (Ret.), my go-to sources for army info, thanks for your love and support. I'm indebted to Trina L. Mitchell, CPT (Ret.), Medical Corp, U.S. Army; and Nikkia Y. Russell, 42A, U.S. Army SSG (Ret.) for sharing thoughts about their experience as African American women joining the army. Christine Taylor-Butler, thanks for moral support; Claire Rudolf Murphy, for manuscript feedback and friendship. To all my amazing, supportive friends in the writing community, especially Mary Douthitt, Meghan Sayres, and Rachel Hamby—you're the best! From the bottom of my heart, a huge thanks to all you readers, librarians, and teachers. I couldn't do this without you.

With love to my favorite, Mike. Thanks for loving me and supporting me always, in everything.

Index

Note: Page numbers in *italic* refer to illustrations